Drama Ministry

Drama Ministry

**practical help for making drama
a vital part of your church**

steve pederson

WILLOW CREEK RESOURCES

ZondervanPublishingHouse
Grand Rapids, Michigan

A Division of HarperCollins*Publishers*

Drama Ministry
Copyright © 1999 by Steve Pederson

Requests for information should be addressed to:

ZondervanPublishingHouse
Grand Rapids, Michigan 49530

Library of Congress Cataloging-in-Publication Data

Pederson, Steve.
    Drama ministry : practical help for making drama a vital part of your
church / Steve Pederson.
            p.   cm.
        ISBN 0-310-21945-0 (softcover : alk. paper)
        1. Drama in public worship. I. Title.
BV289.P43 1999
246'.72—dc21   99-21608
                                                                              CIP

Interior design by Melissa M. Elenbaas
Illustrations in chapter 8 by Mark Demel

Printed in the United States of America

00 01 02 03 04 05 /❖ DC/ 10 9 8 7 6 5 4 3

To Kathy, my partner in life for almost thirty years. I would not be at Willow Creek if you hadn't been willing to leave a tenured faculty position, believing that God would provide (which He has). Your willingness to risk your own career will always be my primary example of love and faith.

Contents

Foreword

The only thing worse than no drama is ... BAD DRAMA!" That phrase has become one of the common sayings in the leadership culture of Willow Creek, probably because in our twenty-three-year history we have seen our share of bad drama! From the launch of our first service in a suburban movie theatre, we have included drama almost every weekend. Our instincts told us that this art form could effectively communicate God's truth because it was obvious that our generation was nuts about movies, television, and live theatre. We had enthusiasm and a few willing volunteers, but no experience with crafting drama sketches for church services and no role models we knew of to learn from. In our youth and naïveté, we boldly began experimenting with drama, hoping to figure it out along the way. The inevitable result in those early years was a few brilliant moments when it all seemed to work, mixed in with a lot more weeks when we concluded that drama in church was a risky business!

When I began serving as the programming director of Willow Creek in 1984, I was deeply grateful for the men and women who had faithfully written, directed, and performed sketches every week. I also realized that we desperately needed to find someone outside our team who could lead us to our next steps as a drama ministry. One of my biggest answers to prayer after a long search was the discovery of Steve Pederson, then a college professor leading a theatre department at a Christian college. I will never forget how God strengthened my faith by leading Steve and his wife, Kathy, to leave tenured faculty positions, uproot their daughters, and come to join our team.

These days drama provides many of the most powerful moments our congregation experiences together. We cannot imagine church without it. This book is the result of the twelve-year investment Steve Pederson has made in helping our church and other local churches around the world to build vital, highly effective, and lovingly led drama ministries. I am thrilled that this book is filled with so much wisdom and practical advice. How I wish a tool like this had landed in my lap when we started Willow—we would have endured far less bad drama!

Finally, I am delighted that this book reflects so accurately the character of its author. Steve Pederson is a man of high integrity who has always led with humility and grace. He wrote these pages motivated by a deep passion for the potential of drama, for the team he so carefully shepherds, for the redeeming power of the local church, and for his own personal love of his Creator. The members of Steve's drama team are crazy about him, and so are all of us who have the privilege of crafting services together. I count his friendship as one of God's best gifts to me, and I celebrate this book as a gift to Christian artists everywhere who agree with us that drama in church can be a beautiful thing.

—NANCY L. BEACH
PROGRAMMING DIRECTOR
WILLOW CREEK COMMUNITY CHURCH

Acknowledgments

I am indebted to Nancy Beach, director of programming at Willow Creek Community Church. Much of what I know about the importance of community and a nurturing style of leadership I have learned from her. I am also thankful for my pastor, Bill Hybels, whose vision for a different kind of church and belief in the power of the arts has given drama a platform to impact the church worldwide.

I am deeply grateful for Mark Demel, my friend and colleague, who has shared leadership of the drama team with me for the last seven years. He has been a blessing to me, our team, and our church.

Willow Creek's drama ministry owes much of its success to our writers, Judson Poling, Sharon Sherbondy, Donna Lagerquist, and Mark Demel. I could not ask for a more committed and talented team. They model humility and servanthood, inspiring me on a weekly basis.

Without the drama team there would be no drama at Willow Creek. I recently tallied the total number of years that this incredible group of people has served on the team. I came up with an astounding 206 years! In terms of commitment and quality, they set a new standard for the word "volunteer."

I am very thankful for my daughters, Kimberly and Kristin. They have been my greatest challenge, my greatest joy. Also my best critics.

Thanks also to my editor, Jane Haradine, at Zondervan. She made me a man of fewer words with an active, rather than passive, voice.

I want to express my appreciation to my sister Nancy and her husband, Gregg, as well as to Jerry and Jan Kehe for providing beautiful lakeside settings for writing large portions of this book.

And last, I thank God for my father, Irvin, whose belief in me and in what I do has provided encouragement all along the way. He has looked forward to the release of this book more than anyone else.

one

The Power of Drama

Drama in the church is not a new phenomenon. As early as the tenth century, short dramatic scenes were incorporated into the mass of the Roman Catholic Church. One of the first recorded playlets, the *Quem Quaeritis*, depicted the three Marys visiting Christ's tomb after His resurrection. The appeal of drama, as strong in the Middle Ages as it is today, gradually led to more and more of the mass being dramatized. In the fourteenth century, drama production within the church had grown in scope and, for the most part, was moved outside the church walls. However, realizing drama was a means to teach the biblical record to a nonliterate laity, the church maintained control over much of play production into the sixteenth century.

The church's view of theatre was not always so positive. Centuries earlier (A.D. 533), it was the church's attack on the morally corrupt Roman theatre that eventually succeeded in stopping formal theatre activity. How ironic that this same church, some four hundred years later, resurrected drama to serve its own ends! But as drama grew increasingly secular, the church began again, as it had in the past, to struggle with it. The early Puritans, especially suspicious of theatre, wielded enough influence in the seventeenth century to once again quell theatre activity.

Since that time, the relationship between church and theatre has often been a rocky one. Any Christian involved in drama has experienced some of the struggle. Back in the 1970s I was teaching at a small Christian college in Iowa and leading a drama performance group that traveled to different churches. The actors and I were often relegated to the church basement (drama couldn't be done in the sanctuary!) and would frequently be required to perform after church (a drama presentation couldn't be incorporated into a worship service!). I recall frequently being weary of the battle. I felt I had to fight so hard for the right to do what I believed God had called me to do that by the time I got "permission" to do it, I had little energy left for the task.

Thankfully, for the most part, things have changed. Today, as we approach the twenty-first century, much of the church is once again embracing the value of drama. In fact, one can argue that we are experiencing a true renaissance of this art form in the church. However, though drama is being accepted, most churches lack the initiative to launch, in a serious way, a drama ministry. Oftentimes drama is merely regarded as something the "young people" do. While most church leaders could not conceive of the notion of no music in the church, they think of drama as merely a nice add-on.

In a little book called *Christianity and Theatre,* Murray Watts writes, "Drama ... has become the dominant form of artistic communication in the western world."[1] One might argue, "Watts is a theatre person, so of course he would believe this." But even if we grant Watts a bit of prejudice in calling drama *the* dominant form, no one would argue the fact that drama is *a* dominant form of communication. To see the extent to which drama arrests the imagination of people worldwide, just look at the multi-billion-dollar movie and television industries. Drama is a major form of communication that people like and respond to, and it's misdirected for the church not to take it seriously. The bride of Christ is called to communicate His truth to a desperately needy world, yet too often we leave out of our arsenal one of the most significant and effective forms of communication known.

The "E" Word

The problem for some who oppose the use of drama in the church is the idea that drama is merely "entertainment." These people assert that "the church should be about the task of saving souls, not about entertainment."

Yes, drama is entertainment, but this fact does not need to be a negative—even in church. Those who object to "entertainment" in the church usually have a limited definition of it. To them it connotes that which is cheap, glitzy, and worldly—the worst of Las Vegas.

> Drama has become the dominant form of artistic communication in the western world.
>
> —MURRAY WATTS

But entertainment can also be truthful and enlightening. Good drama can bring out wholesome laughter or move us deeply. Entertainment for entertainment's sake has no place in church, but entertainment that touches someone's heart and makes that person more open is not only valid, it is desirable.

Another group, while not opposed to drama in the church, views it as appropriate only for those churches that have a more contemporary edge, those that are "seeker focused." Drama, they argue, shouldn't be part of a traditional worship experience because at the core, worship and entertainment are antithetical. Any element that hints of "entertainment" is labeled inappropriate. But isn't a Bach organ piece or a Handel choral work in a more traditional service entertainment? It's time that we set aside the entertainment issue and get on with the task to which we are called—to present the Good News with as much energy and creativity as possible!

The Power of Drama to Break Down Defenses

One of the qualities of drama that makes it particularly important to the church is that it effectively reduces people's defenses. Peter Brook, a famous English director, writes about drama's potential to lay bare what lies in every person that which daily life covers up.[2]

Believers and seekers alike come into churches all over the world, week after week, year after year, wearing smiles but with their defenses up, pretending life is better than it is. However, drama that creates identification can break through those defenses. Drama stirs our memories, probes our psyches, and exposes our pain. It has the potential to create a "lump in the throat" kind of recognition. Perhaps something in our past, or in the present, has been buried psychologically. Done well, even a short sketch can bring that difficulty to the surface. Drama exposes us; it reveals to us afresh just how far we fall short.

> **Drama stirs our memories, probes our psyches, and exposes our pain.**

Drama has the power to unlock that which has been repressed. Let me give you an example. A few years ago, we did a sketch called *A Nice Guy* at Willow Creek. In this sketch, the main character ends up in a classroom in a school he had gone to as a child. As he's looking around, he remembers how he and others in the class cruelly picked on a kid who was "different and talked funny." He painfully recalls an incident when their teasing took a terrible turn. The character is especially disturbed by the memory because he has recently learned that the kid picked on so many years before has committed suicide. Feeling responsible, the man is filled with regret and guilt.

A short time after the performance ended, I happened to run into one of our actors. When he saw me, he started weeping. I put my arms around him, but could hardly console him. Eventually he was able to tell me that while watching the sketch he had a sudden recollection of a similar cruelty that he had taken part in as a child. He remembered how he and some friends had viciously teased a classmate. One day they pulled his pants down and threw him into the girls' bathroom. My friend said that as he watched the sketch and began to recall what he had been a part of, he could hardly stay seated. He wanted to bolt from the auditorium, afraid he would be embarrassed by the flood of emotion he was feeling. When he saw me, it all came pouring out. And this man is one of the last people from whom I'd expect such a reaction. Such is the power of drama.

Years ago we performed this same sketch at a conference in Paris. Following the session, an American missionary came up to me and said, "That was the single most powerful experience I have ever had with drama." The son of missionaries, he said he had grown up in a boarding school and, over the years, he too had done some terrible things to various classmates. So terrible, he confessed, that he had never told anyone about them. As he watched the sketch, he said, he was profoundly moved as the memory of actions from many years earlier suddenly overwhelmed him. And this was all in response to a sketch only eight minutes long!

Just recently, at a Willow Creek Church Leadership Conference, the drama team performed a comic sketch highlighting the challenge of two people trying to make a life together. The sketch begins with a recently engaged couple who are thrilled by the fact that "he/she is so different!" Then, through a series of short scenes covering years of marriage, the characters show how those differences become not only annoying but downright frustrating, at times even infuriating! At the end of the sketch, after a crisis, the comedy turns tender. The husband approaches his wife and says, in essence, that while the two may have their struggles, "I'm not going anywhere." To which the wife responds, "Neither am I." Following is a portion of a letter we received a few days after the conference ended:

> I can't tell you how much this conference has impacted my life. I was told by others who had been here before that

it would be a life-changing experience and it certainly has been that. . . .

. . . The use of drama is so new and "nontraditional" for most of us that I fear it is not easily accepted. However, the power of this form of presentation certainly spoke to my heart Thursday.

In June my wife and I will celebrate our 25th anniversary. But I must tell you that on Wednesday, as our group traveled for 15 hours on a bus to get here, I was working out the financial arrangements for a separation agreement. Our marriage had been rocky at times, but always retrievable. Not this time, I thought. I was *not* praying for God to "fix" it. I didn't want it fixed! I wanted out. But after all the events of the day and the awesome move of the Holy Spirit following the husband and wife sketch, my heart was melted. Through the power of the Holy Spirit it spoke prophetically, as if I was the only person in the room. Thank you for your obedience in following the Spirit's prompting.

Please relay to your ministry team, especially the actor and actress, that Thursday evening when I called home, I told my wife of nearly 25 years, once again—"I'm not going anywhere!" Thank you for your ministry and for what the Lord through you has done for me.

Of course, it's wonderful to get a letter like that. And it's but another reminder that drama, even that which is lighter and less serious, can be used by the Holy Spirit to effect change.

Certainly drama is not the only element in a service that breaks through people's defenses. A song, a sermon illustration, a testimony can have a similar impact. However, drama that reflects real-life experience has the potential to break through defenses very effectively. And if communication is to truly penetrate one's heart, defenses *need* to be conquered.

The Power of Drama to Inspire Worship

Drama at Willow Creek is used primarily in our weekend outreach services, which we do not consider "worship." (Our worship service, New Community, is midweek.) This has caused those who create a more traditional worship experience to believe that contemporary drama is not for them. But this is a far too limited view. Drama also serves a more traditional church because, by breaking through people's defenses, it prepares hearts for worship.

There are perhaps as many definitions of worship as there are worship leaders. But a definition I find particularly helpful is: "Worship is seeking to understand who God is, who we are, and responding appropriately." If we accept this as a working definition, then understanding who we are is a crucial part of worship. And drama can assist us in doing this. A sketch like *A Nice Guy* as part of a traditional worship service confronts us with our need for forgiveness and

> **Contemporary drama, by breaking through people's defenses, prepares hearts for worship.**

shows us once again how desperately we need the grace of God. The point is, there is no authentic worship without vulnerability. We may go through the motions, but if our defenses are up, if we're not open, we cannot experience God.

The Sketch Approach to Drama

There are many valid approaches to drama in the church, running the gamut from sketches (biblical and contemporary) to dinner theatre to major productions. While I believe this book will be helpful whatever approach one takes—the principles are the same, whether directing a sketch or an Easter musical drama—I am a strong advocate of the sketch format.

Willow Creek's approach to drama is to use a six- to eight-minute contemporary sketch (comic or serious) to introduce the topic the pastor will address. A good sketch creates a high degree of audience identification. While biblical sketches can be effective, we are strong proponents of contemporary drama that reflects the real world, the world people live in. This is the kind of drama that has the potential for the most identification. The goal is to raise questions and create tension without giving answers.

I believe the sketch format (we don't like the word "skit"— that's what camps do) is the most accessible approach to drama for churches of any size. A few props, no elaborate sets, a couple of actors, a few hours of rehearsal, and you're on your way!

Well, it's not quite that easy. Thus the rest of this book.

Why Drama's Potential Is Unrealized

It is exciting that churches today are more serious about using drama, but in their enthusiasm to jump on the "drama band-wagon," many are making mistakes. If programs are launched with unclear vision and a lack of understanding of how good drama is created, then those programs will be, at best, minimally effective, and, at worst, short-lived. I'm always discouraged by the pastor who says, "We tried drama, but it didn't work for us." I want to say, "Maybe you weren't going about it as effectively as you could have." If drama is to ever truly gain a solid foothold in the church, we need to stop making the same mistakes over and over.

Lack of Skilled Leadership

The biggest obstacle to raising the quality of drama in the church is lack of skilled leadership. There are many well-intentioned people who love drama and want to see it used in the church, but who lack the knowledge and skill to do it well. I believe this happens more in drama than in the other arts because, of all the arts, drama seems the easiest. The scenario goes like this: A lover of the arts wants to serve the church. While it is very clear this person cannot play the piano, or sing, or dance, talent in drama is more difficult to measure—at least initially. This well-meaning person says, "I think I could act, or even direct. How hard can it be?" Thinking like this is wreaking havoc on church drama ministry. Church leadership, anxious to have a drama ministry, frequently takes the same attitude and too easily grants permission to an enthusiastic but virtually no-skills neophyte to lead the charge. Every time this happens, the cause of drama in the church takes a big step backwards.

Like any art form, there is much skill that goes into creating good drama. When drama works well, one is never conscious of the actor or the director's skill, rather one simply believes what is being seen is real. Samuel Coleridge called this "the willing suspension of disbelief." In a good sketch, an audience is caught up in the characters, the action, and the tension and is unaware of the techniques used to achieve such believability. In fact, more than any other art form, the methodology of drama is, to the uninitiated, difficult to discern. Thus the problem.

The biggest obstacle to raising the quality of drama in the church is lack of skilled leadership.

To those who love drama but lack the knowledge and skill to do it well, I say, "Get some training." A person doesn't necessarily need a theatre degree, but some courses in directing and acting, possibly also playwrighting, will prove very helpful. Such classes can be taken at liberal arts colleges and community colleges on a per class basis. Many professional theatres also offer these kinds of classes. If a potential drama director needs some training, it would be a wise investment for a church to help make it possible by paying tuition, and perhaps even child care if that is needed. Church leadership needs to set the mark high and not be content with shoddy drama. The problem, however, is that too often churches are more intent on getting a drama program going than they are with making sure whoever leads the ministry is qualified.

In addition to formal training, involvement in organizations such as CITA (Christians in the Theatre Arts, see Professional Organization/Training in Appendix) can also be helpful. This organization provides numerous regional conferences and one national conference each year. The training and encouragement provided by networking and workshop opportunities at such conferences can be very valuable. Furthermore, The Willow Creek Association and other denominational organizations annually provide drama training through workshops and conferences.

The Value of Critique

Beginning directors can get a great deal of help from a mentor. After understanding some basic principles of acting and directing, as simple as it sounds, one learns by doing and by having work critiqued and evaluated. In a drama class, there is much critiquing and evaluating of a student's work by the instructor and the other students. A mentor, someone with more experience, can provide that critique for a church drama director. Finding such a person is not easy. Perhaps a respected teacher is asked to function in this role. Some payment might be involved. The mentor may not even be a believer. It's better to have an eminently qualified non-Christian as a mentor than a less qualified Christian. Obtaining objective outside feedback from someone "who knows" is invaluable. Without such feedback, we're likely to create work that is less than it could be.

Inviting and then accepting a critique can be difficult. It's important to look at everything we do, whether we've been directing for one year or twenty years, as a learning opportunity. Too often, I fear, our pride and insecurity get in the way, becoming hindrances to hearing and accepting valid critique. If we're to grow in our craft, we cannot let this happen.

I am chagrined by how often I've experienced drama in a Christian context that is not good. Obviously, this feeling isn't shared by the people doing it; they most likely believe that what they are presenting is working. How does this happen? How can one person be embarrassed for the people performing, while the director and performers themselves are taking pride in their work?

As I was preparing for a conference recently, I went back into the archives to pull out videos of sketches we did years ago. The idea was to demonstrate progress made in our drama ministry over the years. This was definitely accomplished. Looking at those early sketches, I had the painful experience of realizing that work I thought was good at the time clearly left much to be desired. The upside of such an experience is that it's obvious we are growing in our craft. The downside is that it's evidence we tend to view our own work as better, rather than worse, than it is.

We must try to remain as objective as we can about what we create. Feedback helps us to do that. Invite feedback from those who have high artistic standards and understand drama. Find a mentor. Network with other respected church drama directors. Share videos for the purpose of critique and not simply a "slap on the back." Don't create your art in a vacuum. As difficult as it is to hear, we all need people in our lives who will honestly tell us when something isn't working and why.

Valid critique also can come from your own team members (pastor, church staff, and volunteers in the arts). While not as objective as an "outside" perspective, it is very valuable nonetheless. At Willow Creek the staff programming team meets every Tuesday morning to critique the previous weekend service. We watch a video of the music and drama portions and all are expected to give an honest reaction. Sometimes the comments about the drama portion are very positive; other times concerns are expressed. Comments like "The actor seemed a bit unnatural" or "The script appeared somewhat flat; it never really pulled me in" are not unusual. If more than one person feels the same way, we try to get to the core of the problem. A critique session is helpful only when you come away with some understanding of what caused a problem. While we all would rather hear "Great job; I was really moved by the sketch," we end up learning more about the craft of drama when comments are less than positive.

Abusing the Art Form

Another deterrent to drama's potential arises from a basic misunderstanding of the nature of drama. Drama works best when it reflects life in all its pain and wonder. Too often, Christian writers preach or try to make a point in a heavy-handed manner. It's not that good drama doesn't have a point; it's simply that the "point," or message, can't be too obvious. Character and situation must remain in the forefront. When Christians talk about "using drama to evangelize" or "drama with a message," they're actually abusing the art form. Good drama doesn't preach. Dorothy Sayers, a great Christian novelist and playwright, said it best, "Playwrights are not evangelists." Years ago I was attracted to Willow Creek's approach to drama because of the potential to keep a clear distinction between art and message. I realized that even though drama consisted of short sketches, the sketches could have integrity as drama because there was no expectation that the drama preach. Rather, drama could be used to create identification with an audience, to expose a problem, to present a "slice of life" in which the audience could readily see themselves. The preaching, so to speak, could be left to the pastor. Such an approach frees drama to do what it does best rather than forcing it to do what it does not do well. The combination of drama presented by actors, with a message given by a pastor, is a terrific "marriage." While the sketch helps people get in touch with an issue or problem, the pastor brings a biblical perspective to that issue.

> When Christians talk about "using drama to evangelize" or "drama with a message," they're actually abusing the art form.

Many of the sketches produced at Willow Creek are in and of themselves secular; in other words, no Christian perspective is presented. This fact has led some to accuse us of being "into entertainment" and of "watering down the Gospel." These people miss the point. Every sketch we do takes on Christian significance when in the context of an entire service. And a message is always a significant part of that service. It's just not part of drama.

Another way the art form of drama is abused is when we "push" to convey a certain perspective and end up with a "melodrama." The term "melodrama" generally connotes a play that is strong on plot and weak on character development. Emotions are exaggerated. There is a clear distinction between good and bad, right and wrong. We laugh at the old nineteenth-century melodramas in which a Dudley Doright hero rescues the heroine and conquers the villain, all in the nick of time. Unfortunately this pattern is still evident in much of television and film today. But it is not a real picture, because it does not take into account the "gray" areas of life. Rather it reduces life to its simplest, most basic form. It presents a world we can easily "get our arms around," a world the way we wish it were. The problem is that life frequently operates in the gray areas and is often hard to figure out. Melodrama makes life seem simpler than it is, and when we resort to it we fall prey to lying rather than being truthful. In melodrama, evil is always punished, good is always rewarded. It doesn't work that way in the real world. In the real world the innocent suffer. In the real world murderers go unpunished.

So what does this have to do with an eight-minute sketch in a church service? If drama is to have an impact, then it must reflect the real world, warts and all. Musicals can get by with making life seem prettier than it is (they oftentimes present the world as we wish it were), but if we are attempting with our drama to bring about life change, we must stay squarely rooted in what is real. If drama makes life seem simpler than it is, we end up losing those who are navigating a very challenging life's course. If we present "pat," simplistic solutions to problems, we defeat those who are overwhelmed by life.

Commit to Being Real

Being real in drama simply means presenting what is true to life. In other words, a given situation is represented with honesty, avoiding making it either less bleak or more bleak than the situation merits. Churches often appear to be uncomfortable presenting the downside of life. Some argue that there's enough that's negative on television and in the evening news without also presenting it in church. Shouldn't the church, they argue, be about the business of uplifting and of edifying its people? They're right, of course. But we also must not avoid the sometimes dark reality of our lives.

> **If drama is to have an impact, then it must reflect the real world, warts and all.**

Frederick Buechner has this advice for pastors who want to have a vital ministry. In his book *Listening to Your Life,* he says:

> He (the pastor) is called to be himself. He is called to tell the truth as he has experienced it. He is called to be human. . . . If he does not make real to them (his congregation) the human experience of what it is to cry into the storm and receive no answer, to be sick at heart and find no healing, then he becomes the only one there who seems not to have had that experience because most surely under their bonnets and shawls and jackets . . . all the others there have had it whether they talk of it or not.[1]

Buechner's advice seems obvious. But, sadly, too many of us in ministry feel we always have to have the answer, that we cannot be honest about our own doubts, fears, and failures. The irony is that if we were to truly be vulnerable about an area of struggle in our life, it would be immensely encouraging to someone else who is struggling with the same issue.

Not long ago my wife and I had dinner with a woman who had experienced a terrible tragedy six months before. She had lost a number of family members in an auto accident. This woman, a strong Christian, talked about what a struggle of faith she was experiencing. She felt alone and alienated from God. Knowing this woman was a long-standing, active member of a church, I asked her if she had people with whom she could be honest and from whom she could find support. I was surprised by her answer. She said that she had not shared her struggle with any of her friends at church for fear that she would be judged or simply told to "read her Bible and pray more." I had a hard time believing this would actually be the case. But there was something in the "atmosphere" of her church that did not allow her to feel safe enough to be real about her faith struggle. She felt she had to pretend and ended up living in isolation. I can think of few things more sad.

Years ago we learned a great lesson about the power and healing that results from being real. We were in a series on prayer, and the last topic was "The Mystery of Unanswered Prayer." At that time we were doing far more comic sketches than serious ones, but we knew that this topic demanded a serious approach. The sketch we developed, written by Sharon Sherbondy, was called *Great Expectations* (reproduced in chapter 6). It was based on the experience of friends of Sharon.

The sketch was about a couple who for years had been dealing with the pain and frustration of infertility, and who were now about to get a son through adoption. They are only hours away from getting their child. They believe their prayers have finally been answered.

Then the husband returns home and tells his wife that the birth mother has changed her mind. They will not be getting their child. The news is devastating for both of them, but the woman is especially broken ... and angry. She is mad at God who "dangles a carrot in front of us only to yank it away." When the husband says, "I don't think this is His fault," the wife responds with, "Whose fault is it then? He's the one we've been praying to all these years."

At the emotional climax of the sketch the woman lashes out: "I hate this ... I hate that girl.... I hate you ... I hate God ... I hate this." She then collapses in her husband's arms. At the end of the sketch the couple is broken, empty. No solutions are offered—any solution would come off as a mere platitude.

Great Expectations is a dramatic example of what Buechner calls the "cry into the storm" that receives no answer. This is reality. I'm sure some have difficulty with such a bleak sketch performed in a church, especially when the central character proclaims, "I hate God." But we have been amazed over and over again by the number of people who have been deeply ministered to as a result of the honesty of this sketch. I recall a woman who came up to us with tears in her eyes and said, "Thank you. That was my story. And I reacted exactly as that woman did." She went on to tell us that her experience happened many years earlier, but that the pain, largely a private one, was still there. She was so grateful because the sketch had validated her emotions, and she felt safe enough with us to confess her own struggle with God.

In his book *Open Windows*, noted author Philip Yancey argues for Christian writers to be real.

> Sometimes when I read Christian books, especially in the fields of fiction and biography, I have a suspicion that characters have been strangely lobotomized. It's as if an invasion of body snatchers has sucked out the humanity I know and replaced it with a sterilized imitation. Just as a lobotomy flattens out emotional peaks and valleys, Christian writers can tend to safely reduce life's tensions and strains to a more acceptable level.[2]

Acceptable to whom? To Aunt Tillie, who has been sitting in the same pew for thirty years? If we write to please her, we will not communicate authentically with the people we need to reach. Yancey goes on to write:

> A biblical book such as *Jeremiah* or *Hosea* spends a full chapter describing, in graphic terms, Israel's resemblance to a harlot who goes a-whoring, sleeping with every nation that comes down the street. We tend to take those same thoughts and express them as "God is mad at us," or "God

is disappointed in Israel." Tragically, we also miss the emotional force of forgiveness that follows such gross adultery.... A perverse fear of overstatement keeps us confined to that flatland realm of "safe" emotions and tensions—a fear that seems incredible in light of the biblical model.[3]

If Yancey is right, and I believe he is, and churches are fearful of going too far, being literally addicted to playing it safe, then ministry potential is greatly diminished. What are we afraid of? The biblical record is on our side. There should be no topic or issue that we cannot deal with honestly in church.

Another one of our sketches, *Hungry Children*, depicts a Sunday dinner with a family around a table. At first it seems like an all-American setting, but it soon becomes clear that the father is verbally abusive to his wife, his young son, and his teenage daughter. The venomous tongue of the father makes the sketch almost painful to watch, so much so that when I first read the script I was concerned about doing it. I felt the father was too much of a brute, and that the whole sketch was a little "out there," certainly not in the realm of "safe emotions and tensions." (I, too, fall victim to wanting to "play it safe" at times). The writer, Donna Lagerquist, assured me that it wasn't as "out there" as I thought; rather it was grounded in experience she knew all too well. With the support of my team we decided to go ahead with it, and I was shocked by the number of people who said, "That was my father."

> **If . . . churches are fearful of going too far, . . . addicted to playing it safe, then ministry potential is greatly diminished.**

The sketch clearly touched a chord with a large segment of our audience, many of whom responded emotionally through identifying with the wife and children or, in some cases, with the father. It is very important that a sketch like *Hungry Children* is followed sensitively, especially if some latent emotion has been tapped into. This could involve a song, some comments, and a prayer, and even a later response by the pastor in the message. This sketch will always be a good example to me of the power of taking risks and of being real.

Less Is More

There seems to be a trend, especially in large churches, to stage elaborate productions, primarily at Christmas and Easter. These are usually ticketed events intended as outreach in a community. While there is nothing wrong with a large-scale production (we do some ourselves), too often the focus is on spectacle instead of on crafting simple heartfelt, potentially transformational moments.

Spectacle relies on arousing interest through elaborate displays. Story and character—the real stuff of drama—are relegated to the backseat. What ends up driving the production are the special effects (everything from falling snow to smoke to Vari-Lites), a huge cast (even animals), and elaborate sets and costumes.

There is nothing inherently wrong with these things, but too many count on gimmicks and big displays to do the job of drama. Broadway for years has relied primarily on the appeal of spectacle to draw an audience. While many are entertained, even experiencing a chill up their spine at an effect, real impact is generally minimal. Rarely does one experience the power of transformational drama and spectacle working together, as you do in what is perhaps the greatest piece of musical theatre ever, *Les Misérables*. And many of the greatest moments in this work are the ones staged simply—the haunting "Bring Him Home" and the wrenching "I Dreamed a Dream."

> A simple story, believable characters— there is where the real power of drama lies.

I fear that too many of us are putting our best energy into creating spectacles—and they do take a lot of energy. We may be providing a kind of "Christian entertainment," but we have to do more than that. We need to get back to a simple story, to real, believable characters, because there is where the real power of drama lies. In some ways, too many of us have been working too hard in the wrong direction.

There's an old adage in the theatre: "Less is more."

It's still true today.

three

Assembling a Team

One of the most rewarding aspects of building a team is the privilege of coalescing a group of talented people for the purpose of doing ministry together. Providing an opportunity for people to use their gifts to serve God, and thereby find fulfillment, is one of the great joys of life.

It is my conviction that there are talented people in every church, regardless of size, who are never "discovered." Often they themselves don't know they have any talent.

Sharon Sherbondy is a perfect example. Sharon is one of the veteran performers and writers at Willow Creek. But twenty-three years ago, she had no drama experience. She was never in a play in high school or in college. She had never had a drama course. Nor did she think she had any acting talent.

Sharon ended up at an audition because a friend needed a ride. During the audition, she waited in a hallway, "acting silly" with others who also were waiting. Someone suggested she try out for the drama team. After much resistance, and mostly on a lark, Sharon did audition. She was chosen for the team; her friend was not. Over the years Sharon has had an amazing drama ministry that has given her opportunities to perform all over the world.

Imagine what would have happened to Sharon if her natural talent had not been recognized and given an opportunity to develop. Think of the huge loss to the church if Sharon's giftedness in drama had never been discovered.

Sharon's story is not unique. Mark Demel, Willow Creek's associate drama director (and a very talented actor), came to the drama team eleven years ago without any previous experience, as did Ted Thomas, a leading performer for twelve years.

The good news is that there are other Sharons, Marks, and Teds out there in churches, large and small, all over the world. They just need to be discovered and then given a chance to grow.

Finding the Talent in Your Midst

Going on a treasure hunt for potential actors can be very exciting, but it can also be very challenging. I learned a valuable lesson in my first job as a director back in the '70s. I had been hired by an inner-city church to work with youth in a summer theatre program. I selected a play to do and then placed audition notices all over the church as well as in the church bulletin. The night for auditions arrived, but no one showed up! Not one person. There I sat, alone, clipboard in hand, with a stack of audition forms.

That taught me about the necessity of going after people instead of waiting for them to come to me. This applies to all ages—young people, college age, and adults. We need to be bold in approaching others about the opportunity to become involved in drama. People love to be asked.

Generally, I look for individuals who have charisma, an ease and naturalness in their demeanor, a sense of humor, and energy. I look for people who appear confident and comfortable with themselves. The person who stands out in a group, the one you notice when you enter a room. Obviously, this method isn't foolproof, for there are those without any unusual appeal who also have great potential as actors.

When you ask someone if they would be interested in exploring a drama ministry, the response is predictable. They want to know why you were drawn to them. Tell them. Express what it was that attracted you. Be honest. Tell them why you think they might have potential. Most people are flattered by such a response and many, if they have any interest in drama at all, will explore the possibilities.

Typically, one holds auditions to find actors. However, since auditions are by nature threatening, especially to those who have never auditioned, it might be best to begin more subtly. Simply have a meeting or, better yet, a gathering in a home to talk about and explore a drama ministry. The meeting would be open to anyone in the church, but you invite some. In the meeting a vision of drama ministry is cast in an attempt to generate enthusiasm. Some scripts can be read to demonstrate the purpose of drama, giving those attending an idea of what a drama ministry might look like. As each person reads from a script, you can get a sense for who might be able, with time and rehearsal, to perform.

A church in England began its drama ministry this way. A group gathered together a number of times and had fun reading various scripts. When a couple of the readers sounded pretty good, the ministry leader challenged them to work on just two pages of script, memorize the lines, and do them for the group the next time they got together. This generally met with some resistance ("I can't do that!"), so the leader as well as others in the group had to be very encouraging. If the "actors" got a positive reaction to what they did at the next meeting, they felt safer and were then willing to risk tackling the whole script. Eventually, the script would end up being performed in church, but it was a gradual process, nurtured through the safety of the group. If actors, in their first performance, have a positive experience, they likely will act again.

Eventually, however, the best way to assemble a drama team is through auditions. But auditioning for a team is not the tradition of most churches. If someone wants to sing in the choir, they do (whether or not they're any good). If they want to act, they do. But if a team is assembled without auditioning, eventually there will be some very discontented and frustrated people. That's because directors will avoid assigning roles to those who are not good. And a nonauditioned team will invariably have these kinds of people.

The better option is to clearly articulate the purpose of an audition. The experience itself will be an eye-opener for some who will come to their own conclusion that acting isn't for them. For those would-be actors who don't make the team, a director needs to say "no" with real sensitivity, being careful to separate talent from person, so the individual doesn't feel devalued.

Sometimes when a person is not invited to join the team, they respond by saying, "But God called me to this ministry." Obviously, this can be challenging. However, the leader, having been entrusted to "make the call," needs to proceed confidently, basing the assessment on what is seen. At the same time, the leader must navigate such responses with great care, perhaps even assisting the individual to more accurately discern God's calling.

Obviously, it is vital for directors to approach auditions prayerfully, with the desire to truly discern God's will. Ministry leaders are in a position to make decisions that greatly affect the lives of other people. Therefore, we must approach the challenge humbly and seek God's direction.

For those who were asked to a callback, or second, audition and still don't make the drama team, I strongly urge the director to personally call them with the news. These people deserve a response from the ministry leader and even an explanation as to what was lacking. It would be easier to just write a letter or pass the job on to someone else, but I believe a phone response from the director is a validation of that person's investment of time and energy.

Accepting a negative decision is easier for those who don't make the team when they know that more than one person was in on the decision. At Willow Creek, both Mark, the associate drama director, and I lead auditions together, and we invite a couple of key drama team members to the final callback. Together we assess the quality of those who audition. Objective input from some perceptive drama team members who did not sit in on the earlier audition is always helpful. We can then go to those who auditioned with a group opinion, a fact which makes a negative assessment easier to accept.

The Audition Process

Auditions are intimidating, even for experienced performers. Imagine, then, how hard it is for those who have little or no acting experience. They know just enough about what is entailed in a tryout to say "No way!" They need encouragement. A lot of encouragement. Assure them that you are aware of the fear factor and you're determined to make their experience an enjoyable one.

Drama directors need to create fun auditions, ones that are as nonthreatening as possible. I don't think it's wise, for example, to ask anyone to bring a prepared monologue to a first audition.

> Create fun auditions, ones that are as nonthreatening as possible.

Many would never show up! It's much more appealing to say, "No preparation necessary." An audition, especially that first audition, needs to be as easy as possible. Don't allow unnecessary psychological barriers to deter involvement.

One way to reduce discomfort in a first audition is to do group activities. Avoid singling out individuals to stand up and read from a script while the rest of the group watches. This is what people fear. My first audition typically never involves an individual reading from a script; rather it's made up entirely of games, a nursery rhyme exercise, and an open dialogue.

At Willow Creek we're primarily interested in assessing three things in an audition:

1. naturalness—people who are real and not "actors,"

2. free spirits—a "go for it" attitude—not being afraid to risk, and

3. flexibility and versatility.

The key is to structure an audition that, in addition to being as nonthreatening as possible, will provide insight into these three areas. After telling those who are auditioning what I'm looking for, I begin with movement exercises that involve everyone (see exercises 1, 2, and 3 under "Movement Exercises," pages 54–55). With everyone doing the same thing together, there is less focus on the individual. It feels safer. These exercises are good for assessing how imaginative and free-spirited people are. Do the auditionees "go for it" or do they stand there a bit embarrassed and "stumped" as to what to do? Once everyone is warmed up, and therefore more relaxed, I move on through the Dream Exercise (exercise 4, page 55), which really "tests" how free-spirited a person is. Everyone participates, which in itself frees people, making them less self-conscious.

For a large part of the first audition I use an exercise I learned many years ago from Frank Whiting, a former theatre professor at the University of Minnesota. The script is a nursery rhyme, "Jack and Jill" or "Mary Had a Little Lamb." A person's flexibility and creativity are tested when the rhyme is said assuming different emotions and characters. I begin with a group of six or eight, standing in a circle with me, and ask each person to say one line of the rhyme. For example, the first person says, "Jack and Jill went up the hill," the next person says, "to fetch a pail of water," etc. (Because these are the first words spoken by individuals in this first audition, I start with just a short line and gradually build to the whole rhyme.) I have them say the line assuming different emotions or states of being: angry, proud, fearful, shy, irritated, sly, as though "in love," as if the "funniest story ever heard," the saddest story.

After having fun with this, I have people say the whole rhyme assuming animal traits. The idea is not to imitate an animal but to use a quality of the animal in how one says and physicalizes the rhyme. They should be encouraged to move around some. This obviously is very good for testing flexibility and how free-spirited a person is. Suggest animals such as an elephant, giraffe, monkey, bear, puppy, snake, cat, ostrich. Again, the idea is not to "become" the animal but only to use a quality of that animal to create a unique, albeit eccentric, character. This usually ends up being great fun, with much laughter, which in turn helps to make those auditioning more relaxed and less tense.

Using the same rhyme, or switching to another, I ask them to assume various characters in a local high school: head cheerleader, burned-out principal, drama coach, football coach, captain of the pompons, girls' physical education teacher, dance instructor, captain of the football team, bus driver, valedictorian. Or I have them do individuals one might find in a small town: policeman, town drunk, waitress at the local greasy spoon, itinerant evangelist, town bully, president of the Lions Club, hardware store owner. For one more layer, I might assign each person an animal and ask them to incorporate that into the character they play. For example, if someone is assigned "captain of the football team" and "bear," then their character should reflect that. While the result might be a somewhat broad characterization, it should still be believable. I offer some suggestions and have them do it again. This gives me an opportunity to see how well an individual responds to and incorporates direction. I usually conclude the audition with Open Dialogue #1, on page 67. This allows everyone an opportunity to work with a short script, assuming different characters. Throughout the whole audition it is important to make sure everyone gets equal time.

From an audition that includes these elements, it is fairly easy to determine who should get a call for a second audition. It's important to thank everyone for their time and tell them that some will get a call for a second audition within a couple days. Always give a specific date for that callback. Make it clear that if they don't get called, it means "we can't use you at this time." Then send a follow-up "thank you" letter to those you don't invite back.

When an audition is enjoyable, you'll often have people come up before leaving and say, "Even if I don't make the team, thanks. I had a great time!" Obviously, that's gratifying to hear. But another important aspect of a fun audition is that it often convinces the more talented, who might be a little "on the fence" and "testing the waters," that drama would be an enjoyable ministry for them. Then, when asked to a callback audition, the majority will enthusiastically accept. A positive audition experience is our most important recruiting tool—all the more reason to make sure that the first experience is as enjoyable as possible.

The Callback Audition

For this audition I don't hesitate to give people a short monologue (a long paragraph). I ask them to look it over and "see what you can do with it." It's important to get a sense for what people can do if they have a chance to work on something, because many are not good cold readers. I stop short of asking them to memorize the monologue, but many do. Since these individuals have already made the "first cut" they have the confidence, even if inexperienced, to tackle a brief monologue.

> **A positive audition experience is our most important recruiting tool.**

Like the first audition, I begin this one with some warm-up games before having the auditionees perform their monologues. Then, for the rest of the audition, we read from scripts, and we test their skills—or "go for it" attitude—on various improvisations (see samples on pages 74–83). It may be necessary to have more than one callback audition. Since the success of your drama team depends on the selection of the team members, don't jeopardize that success with inadequate audition time.

This is only one way to approach auditions. But it's a place to start, the goal being to devise an audition technique that is right for you.

Spiritual Commitment

While talent is essential, one's spiritual life is also a factor in determining team involvement at Willow Creek. When people audition for the drama team, they fill out a form that asks not only about their drama background and experience but also about their spiritual journey and what their involvement has been in the life of our church. We mandate that actors on the team are all believers and are growing in their faith.

After an individual has passed the talent test of the audition, Mark and I arrange to meet with them, usually over lunch. This gives us a chance to get to know them a bit, and they, us. A large reason for meeting is to assess where they are spiritually. We want to make sure they understand grace and have a personal relationship with Christ. Furthermore, we want to probe their character. What is their motivation for being on the team? Does the person seem to demonstrate a humble, teachable spirit? Are they living, as well as we can discern, a God-honoring life? Prior to this face-to-face meeting we often check with previous ministry leaders or small-group leaders who have worked with the individual.

While character is of utmost importance, there is no foolproof method for assessment. Sometimes people are not totally honest. But since character comprises a large part of the discussion, the potential team member is made well aware of the importance of this issue. We are up-front about the fact that, while we don't expect perfection, we do expect compliance with and acceptance of lifestyle and moral issues on which Scripture is clear. If after meeting with an individual we continue to feel positive, we arrange for them to go through an interview with an elder of the church.

As you are selecting members for your drama team, remember that each one will be representing your church in a very visible way. Church staff members may go unrecognized by the people who attend church, but that's not the case with actors and vocalists. They're visible. Their names and their faces are recognized at church and out in the community. A thorough and thoughtful selection process helps to protect the team, the ministry leader, and the church.

If during your selection process a problem with an individual's character or lifestyle is revealed, that person should not be asked to join the team, no matter how talented. While it's hard to turn away talent, especially when you're desperate for good actors, the alternative is risky. The cost can be too high.

In some cases an individual who is talented but struggles with a character issue might be helped in a one-on-one discipleship relationship. While this requires a considerable investment of time and energy, it could be of great benefit to the individual and it might lead to this person being able to eventually join the team.

While Willow Creek's policy is that all performers are Christians, some churches are more flexible on this issue. They consider involvement in the drama team as a kind of outreach. They would accept a person who is a seeker, or at least not hostile to Christianity, and wants to be a part of a church drama ministry. While there may be risks, there is also a great potential for life change.

Talent Attracts Talent

When a drama ministry is in the start-up phase, leaders always wish for more people. This is often true even for established ministries. When numbers are low, and there aren't enough "bodies" to do a sketch, the temptation is to lower the bar, to accept people who are not as talented as one would like, in order to increase the numbers. But this is risky. Obviously quality will suffer, and this can be a deterrent to the more gifted in the group.

Talent attracts talent. When a church launches a drama ministry, it seems logical that the talented in the church will automatically come forward and volunteer. That's not the way it works. Usually. People in your church who have talent for acting are attracted to the drama ministry *if* the presentations they see are done well. That's when they become interested.

Fifteen years ago Rory Noland was brought on staff at Willow Creek as the music director. In the early years, he focused on improving the quality of the orchestra which, at the time, was not very good. Over the years, as Rory was able to attract talented musicians, the orchestra grew stronger. But the going was slow, much slower than he had expected.

Rory was always on the lookout for good string players. I remember him recounting the story of a particularly good violin player. He was very excited about her audition. When he asked her how long she had been attending Willow, he expected her to say "only a short while." Instead she told him that she had been a regular attender for many years. Rory thought, *Where have you been all this time?*

> If our standards are too low, we will never attract the very people we need—the people with talent.

Most likely, she was waiting for the orchestra to get strong enough to merit her involvement. I think this is the case with a lot of people. The truly discerning and talented do not want to be associated with work that is less than excellent. We think they'll come forward and rescue us. Instead, they're waiting for the program to get strong enough so they won't be embarrassed to be a part of it. They don't want to be "guilty" by association. The truth is, if our standards are too low, we will never attract the very people we need—the people with talent.

A small team of talented individuals is better than a larger group with only limited talent. With a smaller team you'll have to decide how often the group can perform and stay healthy. That may be only once a month or once every six weeks. Work within that schedule, then pray for more troupe strength. Building a strong drama team may take longer than you want, but be patient. Don't compromise standards in order to attract more members. A small, but talented, corps of actors who present consistently strong work will attract others. It's only a matter of time.

four

Training a Drama Team

While it's great to have experienced actors on one's team, I enjoy working with people who have little or no drama background. Not all drama training is good. Many so-called trained people have bad acting habits that are very hard to change. Inexperienced people are not hampered by bad habits, and they generally are enthusiastic about wanting to learn how to act.

Training is a vital part of a drama ministry's focus. And this means more than the on-the-job training that comes with doing drama on a regular basis. While this is important, I advocate what is essentially an ongoing class in acting. One learns to act by doing, and the best way to "do" is in a class setting, guided by a teacher who knows something about acting.

Professional actors are always in class—voice class, movement class, improvisation work—it is part of the profession. That's why, if the church is serious about producing drama of professional quality, then we have to be serious about offering training to actors.

When I came to Willow Creek twelve years ago, I was concerned about whether volunteers in a drama ministry would commit to a weekly meeting time largely for the purpose of training (for about one-third of the time the focus is on community, described in chapter 5). But I have found the response has always been a positive one. When people inquire about auditions, we tell them about our Tuesday night class from 7 to

> **Training is a vital part of a drama ministry's focus.**

8:30, saying that it's required that the whole team be there. In twelve years, and talking to literally hundreds of people, I have encountered only a handful of individuals who were not interested in such a commitment. Almost always people are very enthusiastic about the idea of meeting regularly for the purpose of growing in their craft and for community. Frankly, this has surprised me. It's taught me about the importance of "setting the bar high" and not being reticent to ask for significant commitment. People respond.

In the beginning stages of a drama ministry, it may not be possible, or desirable, to offer weekly training. But I strongly suggest that you start somewhere—maybe a workshop once a month or once every six weeks on a Saturday morning. If you work to make these enjoyable, skill-expanding experiences, eventually your actors will be asking you for more training.

Once people agree to the expectation, then it's up to the drama ministry leader to make sure the training offered is worth the time and effort. But here is where we too often fail, offering training

> **The responsibility for keeping a drama team committed to training rests squarely on the leader.**

that seems thrown together and of questionable value. When that happens, attendance drops. The responsibility for keeping a drama team committed to training rests squarely on the leader.

A Training Focus

The first step in training for your drama team is to set a focus. A focus gives something concrete around which to organize the activities of a class, rather than just scheduling a series of acting exercises. In choosing a focus, you need to know where the team members are in their skills and in what areas they need to grow. A single focus can last for a number of months or even through a whole ministry year. Concentrating on a single focus also provides a basis for evaluation of growth. Focus areas for us in recent years have been:

- Being and not acting, performing action that's real.
- Improvisations.
- Physicalization: developing flexibility and working on the physical portrayal of character.
- Playing emotion authentically. How to stay in the moment and not push emotion.
- Character development: moving outside our comfort zones.
- Play cuttings, with the focus on characterization. (Good cuttings from secular plays provide strong material for character work.)

Once I know the focus, then I choose the methods to achieve the goal, such as improvs, theatre games and exercises, play cuttings. I try to go into each training session with more than enough material. Sometimes an exercise falls flat, or doesn't seem to connect, and I'll need to move on to something else. A leader has to be able to read the degree to which the team is involved in a given exercise and respond appropriately.

A training session should be paced like a good script. It needs to move. It needs to be interesting. I try to have everyone active most of the time rather than have the majority on the team just passively observing others. To accomplish this, I often break up the group into small teams, spread throughout the room, and have each team work on the same thing at the same time.

Toward the end of a session we might gather to see what various groups have developed, but often there are no observed "performances."

Without question, the biggest challenge is to devise training that serves the whole team. This is especially difficult when you have a broad range of experience, from the never-been-in-a-play-before to the stage veteran. This is a tall order. While certain acting exercises and improvisations can benefit all performers, whatever their experience or lack of it, leaders need to also provide next step challenges for the veteran team members. For some of your more experienced actors, you could offer opportunities for coaching other actors and for directing. These challenges not only push actors to the next step in their skills, but they also help the church meet the growing needs of the drama ministry. Just remember that creative people need challenge. Otherwise you run the risk that these valued veteran members of the team will get bored and lose interest.

> **A training session should be paced like a good script. It needs to move.**

The following is provided as a kind of "menu" from which you can select exercises for your team to try. Some activities will meet with more success than others. If your team does not appear to be connecting with a particular exercise, switch to another. Be careful, however, not to switch too soon. Novice actors, especially, need gentle encouragement to join an activity. In time, as they grow in their comfort level, they will become more enthusiastic participants. Acting textbooks are another good source for exercises you can use in your training sessions. The Appendix lists additional resources.

Warm-Up Exercises

Zip-Zap-Zog

The object of this game is to pass the sounds in sequence, with energy and speed, to other people standing in a circle. With arms extended in front, slide one palm over the other, "throwing" a "zip," a "zag," or a "zog" to another person through the fingertips. The person responds by passing the next sound in the sequence to someone else. If someone is thrown a "zap," she throws a "zog." Keep it energized and moving quickly. Have fun making it an elimination game. If a person passes a sound out of order, or a wrong sound, he is eliminated. Eventually work your way down to two people in a "play-off." If you have a large number of participants, divide into groups of no more than eight. The champion of one group can play the winner of another.

"Hey" Toss

Again in a circle, or two lines opposite each other, throw a "hey" to another person. Everyone does it at the same time. Use an arm in a tossing motion, as though throwing the sound out of one's mouth. Switch to the other arm. Now kick the sound out using first one leg, then the other. Now use both an arm and a leg, etc. Explore pitch range by using lower pitched "heys," then higher pitched ones. A simple exercise like this is a good way to get the voice and body loosened up.

Stretch, Yawn, Shake

Stretching and yawning are the body's natural means of relaxing and getting rid of excess tension. Do a series of big, over-the-head, arm stretches, moving into yawns. Release the whole body into the stretch. Really go for it. One can also add vocalizing with "ah." Take the body through some shaking motions, as though shaking away tension. Start with the wrists, then to forearms, shoulders, legs, etc.

Aw-er-ee

This is a good vocal warm-up. The pitch of the "aw" is deep, in one's chest. The "er" is the more normal pitch range, the "ee" high. Stand with head tipped slightly back, with mental focus on the chest, and release with a deep "aw" sound. As the head is moved to an upright position, change sound and pitch to "er," focusing on mouth area. Now tip head slightly forward and release on an "ee" sound, in one's higher pitch range. The focus should be on the nasal and forehead area, as though the sound emanates from there. Glide the sounds together, going directly from sound to sound, pitch to pitch. Repeat this series a number of times.

Spine Release

This is another good vocal and physical warm-up. Stand with hands stretched overhead and release tension by isolating, in sequence, various parts of the body. First drop just the wrists, then the forearms, then drop the arms completely with the shoulders, now drop the head forward, now the chest area, finally bend over at the waist, dropping the head toward the floor. With each release motion, the point of concentration should be on letting go of tension in that particular body area. With the releases vocalize an "ah." When completed, return to an upright position, again with arms over head. As this is done, vocalize an "ah" in an ascending (low to high) pitch scale. Repeat a few times.

NOTE:

In all these exercises that include vocalization, make sure to maintain enough breath support. Otherwise the voice will be pushed and "in the throat," rather than a nice, open sound.

exercises

Attacker/Defender

This is a great physical warm-up, which always produces a good response. It is a lot of fun and really gets the blood flowing. With the group standing, have each person pick one person who is their "attacker" and another who is their "defender." No one tells any-one who they've chosen. When the leader says "go," everyone moves so that their defender is always between them and their attacker. The larger the space the better, because the movement can become very frenetic. After a short while, the leader says "stop" and asks everyone to pick another attacker and defender. The game is then repeated. This can go on as long as it stays inter-esting and the group is enjoying it.

Machine

One person begins some broad, rhythmical, machine-like action and vocal sounds to support it. The group should be small to moderate in size. One by one the other members of the group join the first, physically and vocally connecting with the others. Together they create a large machine moving in sync.

Sponge

The group lies down on the floor, then, as the leader counts to ten, each member of the group gradually tightens up his/her body, ending in a kind of fetal mass. This is held for a few sec-onds, then again, on a count of ten, they release back to the orig-inal position. Repeat, each time lingering for a few seconds in the released state. This exercise can be varied by tightening/releasing isolated parts of the body, i.e., arms, torso, legs.

Tensing, Wiggling, Relaxing

With team members lying on the floor, the leader says, "You are tensing your toes." The team tries to isolate their toes and make them tense. The leader continues through other parts of the body: feet, ankles, calves, knees, thighs, buttocks, lower back, stomach, rib cage, fingers, wrists, lower arms, upper arms, upper back, shoulders, neck, jaw, tongue, cheeks, nose, forehead, scalp. The exercise is repeated with "You are wiggling your _____" and "You are relaxing your _____." It isn't necessary to go through all body parts each time.

Floating

There are various approaches to this tension-ridding exercise, which largely relies on one's imagination to induce a sense of relaxation. Since a person is relying totally on one's imaginative strength in these exercises, it's important to take adequate time. Some people will have more success than others. Encourage the team that while these may appear to be a little "out there," it's very important to frequently, in different ways, exercise the "imagination muscle," since it is one of the actor's major tools.

1. With the group lying on the floor, the leader has the team focus on various joints—ankle, knee, pelvis, shoulders, elbows. The idea is to imagine helium filling a joint, giving that area a "lightness." As enough joints are filled, eventually the body begins to float.

2. Individuals lie on the floor with arms outstretched and their legs slightly apart. They imagine that a wall meets their hands and their feet. When they feel the support of these walls, the floor gradually recedes and they float effortlessly, totally supported by the walls and a "pillow" of air.

3. The group gets comfortable on the floor, lying on their backs. The leader helps them imagine a huge white fluffy cloud beneath them. The cloud gives them a great sense of well-being and support. Imaginatively they float, suspended in air.

Concentration and Imagination Exercises

Passing Object

The team sits cross-legged in a circle on the floor. A simple object is passed around the circle. The person beginning the exercise calls out a letter from the alphabet. As the object is passed, each person has to name an object that begins with that letter. Keep the object moving quickly around the circle. The game is not as easy as it sounds.

A variation would be for one person to name a specified number of objects that begin with a certain letter as the object is being passed around the circle and before it gets back to them. The number of objects required will depend on what is realistic, yet challenging, considering the size of the group and how long it takes to pass the object around. The person who previously played now calls out a letter and the next person in the circle plays.

Describe Object

The leader assembles a number of interesting objects, i.e., an umbrella, a baseball cap, a tacky silk flower arrangement, a fly-swatter, etc. Each person in turn takes an object and, while looking at it, describes it in as much detail as possible.

Object Story

Instead of describing an object, tell a fictional story involving the storyteller and the object. Take it slow. Avoid leaping into an improbable situation. Instead, encourage the team members to believe in what they are saying.

Group Story

A group sits in a circle. One person begins to tell a fictional story. At a certain point the leader says "next" and the story is continued by the next person in the circle. The story proceeds in this manner around the group, with the last person providing the conclusion. This is a good concentration and listening exercise, for it forces people to logically build on what has been said previously.

Mirror, Mirror

There are numerous variations to the mirror exercise. The team is divided into partners who stand looking at each other. One person, the mirror image, tries to copy exactly the posture and expression of the other. Partners alternate doing the mirror image. The leader may want to suggest attitudes, i.e., conceited, bashful, afraid. Or different characters: model, professional wrestler, cowboy, lost child, clown, farmer, evangelist, rock star, politician, used car salesman, game show host. A simple exercise like this accomplishes a number of things. It develops concentration and observation skills as well as physical expression. It also helps conquer self-consciousness, which sometimes occurs when either looking closely at another person or when one is looked at closely.

Newspaper

This game is good for exercising imagination. The team is divided into lines of four or five people. A stack of newspaper is placed at one end of each line. The first person grabs some paper and uses it as an object other than a newspaper, i.e., an umbrella, a spy glass, a cape. Once the function is established, the paper is passed to the next person in line, who has to use it as something else. When the last person is finished, the first person moves to the end of the line, and the second person starts the exercise again.

Movement Exercises

#1 Physical Expression

Have the group move around in a manner that indicates one of the following states of being: confident, shy, angry, frantic, depressed, embarrassed, irritated, violent, deranged, bloated, pompous, anxious, carefree, fearful, sly, etc.

Add some less concrete words: slick, balanced, round, dry, heavy, brittle, airy, antiseptic, expansive, acid, damp, elastic, angular, inappropriate, staccato, cornered, piercing.

After exploring different movements for a while, have the group freeze in a *broad* physicalization of some of the words. The word should be explored physically with different movements while the leader counts to three. When the leader says "freeze," all movement stops. Then request the group to explore the same word again, this time making it "bigger." Encourage the team to take risks, be creative, i.e., "Make it bolder. I want to see the epitome of shy. You want to totally disappear."

A variation of the above involves having the team stand in a line. The person at the beginning of the line is the only one to physically represent a word. Again, the object is to make it a broad, larger-than-life, physical representation. The next person in line faces the first and copies her frozen expression. As he turns to the next person, he adjusts his body position while still trying to maintain the essence of the word. This continues down the line, with the last person moving to the front of the line. This person starts the exercise again, responding to a new word.

#2 Physical Adjustment

Have the group move around the room as though limited by the following: size 20 shoes, a nose that's 2 feet long, a head full of helium, a 30-pound weight on the end of one arm, knees that rotate 360 degrees, a 50-pound weight attached to one's rear end, shoulder blades that are three feet apart, a body covered with hair 3 feet long.

The first time through, have the team drop one physical adjustment when another is mentioned. The second time through make the physical adjustments cumulative (size 20 shoes *and* a nose that's 2 feet long, etc.) so that everyone ends up a contorted mess!

#3 Carry and Dispose

Mime picking up, carrying, and disposing of various objects. Line the team up at one end of the room. Have them pick up an imaginary object about 5 to 10 feet in front of them and carry it to the other side of the room. Objects such as: a bucket of water, a block of ice, an animal struck by a car, a child throwing a temper tantrum, a bloody knife, a piece of sticky candy, etc. For a variation, have people work in groups of two and together pick up larger objects: a person who has fainted, a live snake, a heavy trunk, a broken bicycle.

#4 Dream Exercise

The leader describes a series of events in the form of a story. The group, working on their own, acts out the story. Here's one example, but you can make up your own:

Begin with the cloud exercise above (Floating, 3).
Encourage the group to relax into the cloud, taking time to get comfortable and imaginatively feel the cloud's support. Now imagine that the cloud begins to fill with moisture and starts to turn gray. Gradually the cloud begins to bounce

your body around, your feeling of well-being is now replaced with concern. The cloud rumbles more and more and begins to envelop you. You feel claustrophobic as the cloud surrounds you, turning black. It begins to rain, your body is pelted with moisture, and you begin to fall. You're falling through the air, panicking, and hit the ocean and go under the water several feet.

But, magically, the ocean is a friendly environment, you find you can breathe under water and you begin to swim around. You enjoy the beauty of the fish, the coral, the sun reflecting through the water. Your sense of well-being again returns. You find yourself in the middle of a school of fish; they are close but never touch you. Up ahead you see something larger. It's a dolphin. It turns around, swimming directly at you. Just as it reaches you it swims under your body, gently touching it. Now it swims along your right side, now the left. Now, from behind, it swims under you. You grab its dorsal fin and the dolphin takes you for a ride. It's great fun. As you hold on, the dolphin heads for the surface and breaks through the water, breaching far into the blue sky. It dives back into the water, going down deep, and again heads for the surface. This happens a number of times.

As the dolphin swims, and as you hold on, you begin to sense that the dorsal fin is changing shape and the body begins to feel different. Suddenly the dolphin turns its head and you realize you are now on the back of a shark! You panic, but hold on as the shark tries to snap you off of its back. You experience a violent jolt and find yourself flying through the air. You land on a white sand beach and realize you are safe.

The sand is warm and comfortable. You're exhausted, but lying on the sand feels great. The sun warms your body. The temperature is perfect. Your feeling of well-being is interrupted by a bug bite on your left leg. You swat at it. A short while later, another bug bite, this time on your right leg. Again you swat at it. Now a bite on your right arm, your left. Gradually, you experience a strange sensation in your left leg. It begins to tingle and starts to spasm. It gets more extreme, and now the same sensation is felt in your right leg. The bug bites have affected your nerves. Your left arm goes into spasms, then your right. Now your whole body. You're flopping around on the sand, unable to control your body!

Suddenly you leap up, jump into the air and realize you can fly. All the spasms disappear and your feeling of well-being returns as you soar through the air.

You hit a wall, fall into your bed. You wake up and realize all you've experienced has been a dream!

An exercise like this allows people to imaginatively experience a wide range of emotions and sensations. Take time in telling the story, with many long pauses. It takes time to "enter into" an experience like this. The exercise could easily last fifteen minutes or longer. Encourage your team to have fun, let go—no one but the leader is watching, and he/she doesn't have to—but at the same time, they should authentically try to enter into the story, responding physically to what they are feeling. The first time through an exercise like this a group will probably be somewhat reserved. Over time, they will become more and more expressive. As child-like as an exercise like this is, adults will enter into it, enjoy it, and benefit from it.

#5 Team Movement

A. In groups of two to five, create the following: fountain, corn-field, tree, assembly line, photograph, bridge, mountain, rush hour, desert, slot machine, prehistoric monster, toll booth, Halloween, fish, flock, ocean, music machine. The groups should avoid talking and simply follow the lead of the first one in the group to start. Abstract vocalizations can also be added. This is a good exercise for relating physically to one another and helps to get over inhibitions with regard to "touching."

B. Again, in groups of two to five, this time the players "ride" an object together, i.e., a sailboat, car, train, water slide, roller coaster, merry-go-round, bobsled. The point of concentration is to allow the object to create the movement. The team works together, feeling the motion as one unit. No discussion should be allowed. Generally, one or two will start, with the others following their lead.

C. The team is divided into small groups. One person begins miming a simple activity of their choosing. As the others realize what it is, they enter in, one by one, and assist in the activity. Thus the activity chosen has to be one that can be done by a group, i.e., setting a table, harvesting a garden, building a snowman, decorating a Christmas tree.

D. Again in small groups the team develops frozen pictures. On a slow count of five the picture is explored by the team. It is frozen when the leader says "freeze." Suggested pictures: nerds at a nerd convention, the Hatfields and McCoys, Bingo at St. Francis Church, fifty-year high school reunion, L.A. earthquake, Jesus healing the paralytic.

Vocal Exercises

"ah, eh, ee, aw, oo"
Stay on one pitch for all five sounds. Repeat numerous times on different pitches.

"who-who-who"
Explore with different pitches, same as above.

Readings

To energize one's speech, readings can be helpful, especially ones that lend themselves to enthusiastic expression. A piece such as the following from *Yertle the Turtle and Other Stories,* by Dr. Suess, can help a person who might lack energy and expression:

Then the feathers popped out! With a zang! With a zing!
They blossomed like flowers that bloom in the spring.
All fit for a queen! What a sight to behold!
They sparkled like diamonds and gumdrops and gold!
Like silk! Like spaghetti! Like satin! Like lace!
They burst out like rockets all over the place!
They waved in the air and they swished in the breeze!
And some were as long as the branches of trees.
And still they kept growing! They popped and they popped
Until, 'long about sundown when, finally, they stopped.¹

Such a reading can also be used to push an actor into using the full pitch range of his voice, as can the following passage from Jeremiah (4:23–26 KJV):

I beheld the earth, and, lo, it was without form, and void; and the heavens, and they had no light. I beheld the mountains, and, lo, they trembled, and all the hills moved lightly. I beheld, and, lo, there was no man, and all the birds of the heavens were fled. I beheld, and, lo, the fruitful place was a wilderness.

Articulation/Pronunciation Exercises

Tongue twisters are good for developing clear articulation and pronunciation. Amateur actors frequently have "lazy tongues" and are sloppy articulators. Tongue twisters can also benefit pitch variation, i.e., when one is said using chest tone (lower) or head tone (higher).

Peter Prangle, the prickly, pringly pear picker, picked three pecks of prickly, prangly pears from the prickly, prangly pear trees on the pleasant prairies.

Big black bugs brought buckets of black bear's blood.
A big black bug bit a big black bear.

Better buy the bigger rubber baby buggy bumpers.

A tutor who tooted the flute, tried to tutor two tooters to toot.
Said the two to the tutor, "Is it harder to toot
Or to tutor two tooters to toot?"

Betty Botta bought a bit of butter,
"But," said she, "this butter is bitter.
If I put it in my batter
It will make my batter bitter.
But a bit of better butter
Will make my bitter batter better."
So she bought a bit of butter,
better than the bitter butter,
And, it made her bitter batter better.
So 'twas better Betty Botta
Bought a bit of better butter.

Thomas A. Tattamus took two tees
To tie two pups to two tall trees,
To frighten the terrible Thomas A. Tattamus!
Now do tell me how many tees that is.

Sister Susie went to sea to see the sea, you see,
So the sea she saw, you see, was a saucy sea;
The sea she saw was a saucy sea.
A sort of saucy sea she saw.

Seven shell-shocked soldiers sawing six slick, slender, slippery, silver saplings.

A skunk sat on a stump. The stump said the skunk stunk, and the skunk said the stump stunk.

How much wood would a woodchuck chuck if a woodchuck would chuck wood?

Let the little lean camel lead the lame lamb to the lake.

Should such a shapely sash such shabby stitches show?

She is a thistle sifter, and she has a sieve of sifted thistles, and a sieve of unsifted thistles, because she is a thistle sifter.

"Being Real" Exercises

The following exercises address the major acting challenge—to be real. Actor training must, from the very beginning, hold up this value, essentially for actors simply to "be," rather than to "act." Actors should never push to achieve some emotional response, rather they should only respond to what they feel. Genuine emotion is often unlocked through specific action, thus the following exercises will focus much on "doing."

#1 Do and Be

Have your team, working individually, simply do the following: read a book, write a letter, watch TV, look at a photo album, read mail, read Time, etc. Encourage your team to not just go through the motions but to imagine an actual story they are reading, or to whom are they writing. What are they saying? They should be encouraged to see a particular photo album (how we respond to wedding pictures and to photos of a memorable family vacation after a parent is deceased will be different). Don't allow the team to over-respond facially in order to "project" what they're feeling. This is how bad actors develop! By observing an actor, one might not know what they're reading, but that's okay. What is most important is simply to respond authentically to what one sees or does.

A variation of this exercise would be to explore specific action with different objectives. Prompt the team to change objectives and see how the action is done differently. For example, the action is "packing a suitcase." Have the team mime this action individually, but keep changing the reason why—to go on vacation, to run away, to attend an out-of-town funeral of a good friend. Again, it is important to encourage the team to "just do it," with different objectives, and to not overproject.

Drive a car

>going on vacation
>to work on Monday morning
>to pick up a date

Write a letter

>to graciously get out of a relationship
>to humorously express love
>to witness to someone

Dressing

>for a fire drill at 3:00 A.M.
>to go to class, first hour
>to go on a special date

Sitting

>just to relax
>because you refuse to move
>because you cannot move

Walking

> because you're stalking someone
> because you're being stalked
> to meet your fiancee's plane

Working in the garden

> so that you'll be noticed by a neighbor
> in order to have the straightest row of corn
> to keep the rabbits out

#2

Teams of two perform some simple activities, with the point of concentration being on an object: folding a sheet, making a bed, pushing a car that's stuck, portaging a canoe, moving a large piece of furniture, pulling a heavy sled, moving a fallen tree limb out of the road, a tug-of-war, etc. Teams should be encouraged to "do," don't "show."

#3

Have your team individually respond to physical sensations: headache, stiff neck, head cold, eyestrain, foot asleep, hot, cold, pain in the small of one's back, indigestion, stubbed toe, earache, sliver in finger, canker sore. Through what noted acting teacher Anton Stanislavsky called "sense memory," encourage your team to recall what one of the above feels like to them and respond *only* to that. For example, not everyone gets headaches in the same way or with the same intensity. The stereotypical response might be for one's hand to go to the forehead, but for some people the pain might be in the back of the head. Another might feel a headache behind the eyes, causing the eyes to be watery or a bit strained. It's important for your team to realize that an observer might not be able to tell what it is they are feeling. The difference between a headache and a backache, for example, might not be evident. This is okay. Again, the overarching value is for an actor to simply respond authentically.

A variation would involve focusing on one sense and exploring it in some depth. For example, the sense of "smell." Prompt the team to respond to the following odors: rose garden, sewage plant, dog kennel, bakery, fish market, favorite perfume.

Another variation would be for the leader to describe a sequence of events, which each team member mimes. The "story" would allow for sensory exploration. For example, "You are doing the dishes. The water is too hot, so you run cold water into the sink until it is a more desirable temperature. Feeling around in the water, you prick your finger on a knife. You instinctively put your finger in your mouth. You taste blood, grab a paper towel, and put pressure on your finger until the bleeding stops. You resume doing the dishes. While drying a dish, it slips from your hands and drops to the floor. You carefully pick up the pieces. You resume the dishes, but step on a small piece of glass that gets stuck in your bare foot...." and on the story goes.

#4

Ask the team to "see" the following: a beautiful landscape (personalize it, see a specific one), a deer standing in the woods, threatening storm clouds, falling leaves, the ocean.

All the five senses can be explored in this manner. The leader suggests one of the senses, such as "sight," and a specific environment, "art gallery." The team then explores what they see in that environment. Prompt the team to keep it simple.

sight—art gallery
touch—toy store
smell—walking down a busy street
hearing—riding a bike through the neighborhood
taste—a smorgasbord

A variation would be to simply name an environment and have the team describe what they see, smell, hear, etc. With everyone sitting in a circle on the floor with eyes closed, suggest the environment is an "empty old church." First ask people to describe what they hear. After exhausting that sense, move to another. Suggest the individuals only offer observations on senses they "experience," not ones they simply think of, and to describe them with as much detail as possible. Other possible environments: carnival, new car, baby nursery, restaurant.

#5

Creating authentic emotion/feeling is made easier through action. French director Jean-Louis Barrault, in the early twentieth century, evolved an approach to acting he termed "the method of physical actions." His position was that it was through action, the "doing," that emotion is engaged. An actor, he maintained, should never be concerned about emotion. If the action is right, the emotion will be right. An example of this phenomenon in real life happens when we narrowly escape a car accident.

Assume you are in your car going fifty-five miles an hour down a road when, suddenly, a car from the other direction swerves directly into your lane. You immediately pull the car to the right, driving onto the shoulder, while reducing your speed. You narrowly miss the oncoming car. As you gradually pull back onto the road, your heart is beating fast, you begin to break out in a cold sweat. You feel a sense of panic, thinking, *that was a close one!*

Many would argue that the action of maneuvering the car to safety helped produce the feeling of fear and panic. The rapid heartbeat is connected to the physical response. It is sort of a what comes first, the chicken or the egg, kind of argument. Does one feel fear and respond out of that, or does one just instinctively respond and the feeling of fear follows? Psychologist J. W. Peterson underscores this "action first, feeling second" principle when he

writes on behavior modification. He maintains we need to act ourselves into a new way of feeling and not try to feel ourselves into
a new way of acting. Here are a few exercises that underscore this
strong connection between action and emotion.

Rather than simply physicalize a response to a word, the actors
are encouraged to come up with an action that will create the
appropriate response. Say, for example, the word is "spiteful." An
actor could create a scenario like the following: "My roommate has
an 'addiction' to new clothes and, once again, has stolen money from
my wallet and gone shopping. I've confronted her with this before,
but it has happened again. I'm not going to let her get by with it this
time, so I get a scissors and go to her closet and cut the sleeves off
every one of her blouses. I then take the sleeves and lay them neatly
across her bed—to spite her." It is not hard to see how miming
this action can produce the emotion of "spite." Rather than pretending at "spite" from "out of the blue," specific action is relied on
to produce an authentic feeling.

Take the word "cautious." Rather than just acting cautious,
an actor develops a scenario such as this: "I am a prisoner of war,
trying to escape at night. I have to make my way across a large
field without blowing up a booby trap. I crawl on my belly, inch-
ing along cautiously (probably with a fair amount of fear as well!)."

It's important that each actor is given time to think through
their story, to enter into it. It is often fun for everyone to be working with the same word. Or assign a different word to each actor.
Here are a few more: embarrassed, bashful, frantic, breathless,
awkward, jovial, quarrelsome, irritable, scornful, dazed, apprehen-
sive, violent, exhausted.

Open Dialogue

An open dialogue is a script, usually short, that is quite generic. It is adaptable to many different characters, settings, and situations. Within the limits of a set dialogue, the actors are free to explore character. The exercise demonstrates how meaning is established less by lines and more by how the lines are said.

Dialogue #1

A: Hi.

B: Hello.

A: How's everything?

B: Fine. I guess.

A: Do you know what time it is?

B: No. Not exactly.

A: Don't you have a watch?

B: Not on me.

A: Well?

B: Well what?

A: What did you do last night?

B: Nothing.

A: Nothing?

B: I said, Nothing!

A: I'm sorry I asked.

B: That's all right.

Actors could, on their own, develop the who (who these characters are), the where (setting for the scene), the what (what is happening, what the issue is). Or a leader could assign different settings/characters. Here are some possibilities for the above dialogue: (1) a casual pickup (2) husband A, wife B meeting after a trial separation (3) father A and daughter B after she's been out far past her curfew the night before. The setting is breakfast.

(4) college friends meeting after each suspects the other of dating their boyfriend (5) B about to murder A (6) lovers meeting for only a few moments (7) before a double suicide (8) A about to rob B.

Dialogue #2

A: Where are you going?
B: You know.
A: What do you mean?
B: How many times do we have to have this conversation?
A: What are you talking about?
B: Your blindness amazes me. I don't understand you. I never have.
A: Look, I'm sorry.
B: It's too late.
A: What do you mean, it's too late?
B: I'm tired of you and your tricks. I'm leaving!
A: I won't let you.
B: You won't let me? We'll see about that.

Again, actors could be asked to develop their own who, what, and where. The leader might also encourage them to be bold in their character exploration. The leader could allow for the actors to choose either a serious or comic approach, or the leader could limit it to one or the other. The actors should be reminded that they can use pauses; all lines don't have to follow quickly after the one before. Also, action without dialogue can be explored at the beginning. I've experienced this scene done with a good minute of action before the first line is spoken.

Dialogue #3

I see what you mean.
Maybe.
What are you doing here?

I've got _____
Now?
Why not?
Is this it?
I wish I knew.
That's _____
You're _____
Don't preach at me.
This is going nowhere.

_____

(The actors, if they wish, can eliminate a maximum of one line.)

This dialogue allows for more flexibility. Actors, in teams of two, need adequate time to figure out the who, what, and where, as well as to rehearse. They have the freedom to complete a few lines as they wish. Without lines assigned they may also choose to have one character say two in a row, as though it is one line, i.e., "Don't preach at me. This is going nowhere." With everyone working on the same dialogue, the scenes are performed for the whole group. It is always enjoyable to see how vastly different the scenes are. Leaders should feel free to write their own dialogues and experiment with degrees of flexibility.

Dialogue #4

A: What are you doing here?
B: I brought this.
A: Yes. I see.
B: Good.
A: Now what?
B: Maybe it's time to go.
A: Oh.

I first experienced this dialogue in a workshop led by Tom Long of Friends of the Groom, a theatre company. Teams of two are assigned biblical characters and are asked to memorize the lines. It is up to the actors to decide which character says what lines. After time for exploration and rehearsal, the scenes are presented for the whole team. It is then fun for the team to guess who the characters were. Characters:

Jesus and Judas
Adam and Eve
David and Goliath
Joseph and the innkeeper
Samson and Delilah
Moses and Pharaoh
Others?

Improvisations

Without question, improvisation is the most effective tool for actor training. Many acting teachers use improvisations as their primary technique for teaching acting. Improvisations take on many forms, but always rely on the actors to "make up" the lines. There is no script.

The benefits are numerous. First, improvisation helps actors develop the skills of listening and engagement in the action. Many novice actors essentially wait for their cue lines and then say their line. The risk in this bad habit is to drop character while waiting for the cue. Improvisation makes this impossible, since there is no set cue line. One is forced to listen in order to know how to respond.

Improvisations stimulate creativity. Actors need to be "in the moment." Being absorbed in the action is crucial to good acting. An improv forces this involvement; otherwise an actor will not know how to respond. The actor's own knowledge, intuition, and creativity are needed for an improv to work.

Improvisations allow an actor to experience a kind of real-life, give-and-take dialogue in the context of "performance." Improvs often have a very natural feel because they are spontaneous. They are "real." And, as has been discussed, being real for an actor is of utmost importance.

An improv is a great way to explore and develop character. Many improvs emphasize a clear delineation of character and encourage actors to get "outside themselves" and embody what is often unfamiliar.

All actors have had the horrible experience of facing another actor on stage and not having the faintest notion of what to say. It is inevitable that actors will periodically forget, or "go up," on a line. Improvisations are good practice for thinking on one's feet and making up a line that will fit a particular situation. The more practice an actor has at improvising lines, the better prepared he will be to find his way back to a script when he drops a line.

Basic "Rules" of Improvisation

1. Start immediately.

This does not necessarily mean that an actor starts saying something right away, but rather that the action is entered into immediately. Sometimes the temptation is to engage in "chitchat" in an attempt to "ramp up" as one tries to figure out an approach to the scene. Try to avoid this.

2. Resist being a playwright.

Since in an improv actors write the script, this may seem like a contradiction. A novice might ask, how does one avoid being a playwright? It's avoided by staying in the "here and now" without trying to manipulate the action toward a predetermined end. Though some improvs will assign an ending, even then that shouldn't be one's focus. Rather the actors need to be in the moment, attentive to the action and what one's partner(s) is doing. When this happens, the end takes care of itself.

3. Don't play for the audience.

This is hard to resist. When a funny line gets a big response from the audience, it is difficult not to try to come up with more lines that will get a similar reaction. But when this happens, the focus is outside the action of the scene. There is nothing wrong with humor, but it must be a natural extension of character and action. Developing a scene that the audience will enjoy is not the purpose of an improvisation. Sometimes it's appropriate for the leader to set some parameters to assist actors in avoiding this pitfall. Perhaps the scenes can only be approached seriously (though this, in itself, is no guarantee one will avoid playing for the audience). A leader also can ask the audience to observe but not respond. Over time, when feedback lauds that which is real, true to character and action, rather than that which is funny, the team will get the idea.

4. Be a team player.

It's important to build the scene by agreement, not denial. If your partner asks, "So how's work at the cement factory going?"

It's not appropriate to say, "I don't work at a cement factory, I'm a security guard at Wal-Mart!" Flexibility is key. An actor may have an idea for an approach to a scene, but if her partner goes in another direction, she needs to go with her. It's important to trust and stay open. It's also a good idea to limit the questions (this is too easy) and assume you've known the person for some time unless the improv setup is otherwise.

5. Keep going.

When beginning to learn how to improv, it is easy to get stuck. When a novice actor feels self-conscious and doesn't know what to do next, the tendency is to break character and essentially give up. But it's important to keep going, to stay focused on the action. If a period of time passes before anything is said, that's fine, as long as the actors stay in the moment. Generally, only the leader can stop an improv (unless there is a predetermined end point).

6. Maximize learning.

Improvs are great fun and enjoyable to do and witness. But in order for them to be more than that, the leader should help the team to process what was learned. After an improv, or a few improvs, the leader can ask, "What did you learn? What worked, what didn't work as well? Was there a tendency to play for laughs? Was the emotion pushed, or did it seem natural? Did the characters seem engaged in the action? Were the characters interesting and real?"

When possible, an actor should be lauded for taking risks or exploring a character outside of what he normally does. It's important for both audience and actors to provide feedback so that the learning inherent in each improv session can be underscored.

Improvisation Exercises

Class Reunion (a good warm-up improv)

The situation is a class reunion. Individuals are assigned characters such as:

Most likely to succeed
First to have a baby
Most likely to make a difference
First to make a million
First to get into big trouble
First to win a beauty contest
First to make it to the Hall of Fame
First to withdraw from society
Most likely to party
First to win a Pulitzer Prize

The group members all interact, each with one other person or with a small group. When the leader says "switch," everyone has to find new people with whom to converse.

Where? Who? What?

Each pair of actors (can also be done with more than two players) is assigned a where (locale), a who (character), and a what (the situation, the given circumstances).

For example, the locale could be a city bus terminal. The characters could be a homeless person and a police officer. The situation is that the policeman is trying to remove the camped-out homeless person from the terminal.

An interesting elaboration on this kind of improv is for the actors to switch places. After the improv is completed the first time, the two actors assume the other's roles. The scene is played again, this time going further and heightening the characters.

Another approach is not to predetermine a specific where, who, or what. Instead, numerous locales, characters, and situations are written on slips of paper. Each actor draws a character and each team of actors draws a locale and situation. It's also interesting not to establish the what, but to leave this up to the actors.

Assigned Characters

Actors are in pairs. Assign only characters. The actors decide on the where and what.

private detective and veterinarian
race car driver and professor
minister and Mafia member

Word Improvisations

1. Develop an improv around a word. The word doesn't need to be said but, in some way, it needs to be central to the scene.

stigma
disability
guilt
rejection
rut
stoic
sticky
grudge

This could be a "cold" improv, or the leader could allow the actors some time to develop a scenario.

2. In teams of two, three, or four, assign a series of words. As the actors interact—together they might decide on a "who, what, and where"—they have to develop a character that embodies their word. Try to use colorful, image-producing words. Here are a few interesting groupings:

stigma and irresponsibility
guilt and wet blanket
irrational and disability
rejection and tranquilizer

3. Develop an improv during which three assigned words must be said in any order. The improv, using the three words, needs to make sense. If the improve is done well, the team members who are observing should not be able to tell what the three words were. This improv probably requires the actors to plan a bit before beginning. Challenge the team with words that don't have anything in common, i.e., raspberry, giraffe, Christmas.

To make the exercise more challenging, the leader can require the words to be said in the order given.

4. Divide the team into groups of two. One person in each group is assigned a word and assumes a character to which the word is central. The other person has to play an opposite kind of character, though he/she is unaware of what the word is. Suggested words:

insecure
evasive
pompous
guilty
anxious
giddy, etc.

Join In

A person is selected to start an activity of her own devising, such as washing her car. She does this without speaking. When it is clear what she's doing, someone else is asked to join her in that activity. Dialogue and character now develop around the shared experience. Others can be asked to join in if the action merits it.

Pecking Order

In this improv one person assumes the dominant role, the other is submissive. It is not predetermined which is which. The team should be encouraged to not necessarily follow the stereotype. Suggested characters:

librarian and book borrower
manager and secretary
student and professor
actor and director
waiter and customer
teenage daughter and mother

NOTE:

Watch for connection between body language and assumption of status.

Hats and Props

The leader brings a selection of hats and various hand props. The actors select one item around which they have to develop a character. Interesting "wheres" should be suggested by the leader: Vietnam Memorial, movie theatre lobby, McDonald's, airplane, remote mountain cabin.

Hidden Agenda or Emotion

In addition to assigning a who, what, and where, the leader also suggests a hidden agenda/emotion that will, to various degrees, color the improv. It is not predetermined which character has the hidden agenda/emotion. The degree to which the observers realize it may vary. The hidden agenda/emotion could be largely a subtext. Examples:

stable boy and horse owner
  checking on a sick horse
  stable
  hidden agenda/emotion: to harm

husband and wife
  dressing for a twenty-fifth anniversary celebration
  bedroom
  hidden agenda/emotion: guilt

mother-in-law and daughter-in-law
  first visit after honeymoon
  kitchen
  hidden agenda/emotion: to teach

A variation is to assign each character a hidden agenda/emotion of which the other is unaware.

Physical Adjustment

This exercise focuses on the physical portrayal of character. Though this should be part of any improv, it is the point of concentration for this one. Actors are encouraged to use a physical mannerism that is "outside the box" for them, i.e., a limp, stoop shouldered, a tick. Characters are assigned. The where and what can be assigned or left to the actors' devising.

Vietnam vet and investment banker
rock musician and minister
Greenpeace leader and avid hunter
blackjack dealer and pro football player
construction worker and actor
AARP executive and model

Psalms

Assign psalms to teams of two to four from the group. Together each team has some time to brainstorm a scenario that reflects, in some manner, the psalm. They then perform the improv. Following are some suggested passages:

> Our soul has escaped as a bird out of the snare of the trapper; the snare is broken and we have escaped (Psalm 124:7 NAS).

> I shall take no young bull out of your house. Nor male goats out of your folds (50:9 NASB).

> Your wife shall be like a fruitful vine, within your house, Your children like olive plants around your table (128:3 NASB).

> Let the bones which thou hast broken rejoice (51:8 RSV).

> I am a worm, and not a man, A reproach of men, and despised by the people (22:6 NASB).

At the end of each improv, the psalm is read.

Proverbs

In teams of two, develop an improv that centers around various proverbs:

> A stitch in time saves nine.
> Proof of the pudding is in the eating.
> He who laughs best, laughs last.
> The early bird gets the worm.
> Don't put all your eggs in one basket.
> As you make your bed, so you must lie in it.
> If at first you don't succeed, try, try again.

The actors will need some time to develop a scenario. After the improv it's fun to guess what proverb was illustrated.

Poems

Poems can provide a catalyst for some creative improvisations and can be approached in the same manner as the psalms and proverbs. I've enjoyed using the work of author Shel Silverstein, especially a few from his children's classic, *Where the Sidewalk Ends*.

It's also interesting to assign every team the same poem. I never cease to be amazed at the wide variety of improvs this produces.

Bus Stop

Actors choose a name, an occupation, and an object which they mime carrying. The setting is a bus stop (three chairs). The scene begins with two people who need to interact and use the prop in some manner. After some time, the leader indicates that another actor should join the scene. This third actor has to develop a logical reason to enter. Shortly after his entrance, one of the two original actors, preassigned, has to find a logical reason to leave. As other individuals are asked to join the scene, the person on stage the longest has to exit in a way that makes sense. Thus, except for short periods of time when three are on stage, the improv involves two people.

Encourage the team to focus on character and use the prop as an extension of that character. Interesting physicalization and vocal use should also be encouraged.

Animal Improvs

Animal improvs are a delightful way to discover unique and fun characters. They can be used to augment many of the above exercises or as a primary focus. Actors are assigned an animal. The object is not to imitate that animal, but to take a quality of the animal and use it to develop an engaging character. An actor assigned a mouse might, for example, use a higher pitch and a quick, mincing manner of speech. The actor also might move quickly, in little spurts. The character, while eccentric, should not be overly exaggerated. I like to say that whatever character one develops could be a person you'd meet in a line at the grocery store or on the street. Obviously, an improv like this is excellent for physical and vocal exploration.

In my experience with actors, sometimes a character developed in this improv has found its way, albeit modified, into one of our sketches. I recall one of our actresses who was assigned an "anteater." She, much to everyone's delight, developed an interesting, what can only be described as a "tongue thing." One Sunday morning a few months later the team greatly enjoyed touches of this character on stage.

The list of animals is unending: giraffe, ape, cow, elephant, puppy, cat.

Opening and Closing Lines

An improv team is assigned opening and closing lines. This works best when there is no advance planning. Suggested lines:

We did it.   Leave me alone.

It's over.   You've always been my one and only.

Freeze/Replace

This improv is also a great warm-up. The group stands in a circle. Begin with two people in the center who are assigned positions. They start the improv based on their physical relationship. If they are asked to be holding hands, then that has to be the starting point for the improv. The actors should be encouraged to keep the action physically expressive and broad. When the leader says "freeze," the improvers hold their positions, and another person is asked to jump in. This new actor assumes the exact physical stance and position of one of the original players, selected by the leader. When the leader says "go," a new improv begins, again based on the physical relationship but different from the one before. The key is to keep it fast-paced; each improv is short. As soon as the actors are in an interesting position, the leader says "freeze."

A variation of this exercise allows an actor, rather than the leader, to say "freeze." The actor then jumps in, tapping a shoulder of the actor he wants to replace.

Assigned Positions

Two actors are each assigned a beginning and ending position. For example, they begin sitting on the floor, back to back. They end with one standing on a chair, the other kneeling. The goal is to make sure there is a valid reason for the positions.

In an improv like this, one has to be extra sensitive to what his partner is doing. Actors have to work together as a team.

Interrogation Exercise

A person is assigned a concrete, descriptive "get your teeth into" adjective. Good examples would be irascible, fretful, cornered. Avoid words like fear, happy, sad. Divide into teams of two. One person simply interrogates the other, using a lot of "why" and "how" questions. The interrogated partner explores a character physically and vocally that personifies the word. After adequate time, switch parts and assign a new word. The interrogator becomes the interrogated.

NOTE:

The above exercises and improvisations can be revisited a number of times. It isn't as though once done they can't be done again. In fact, often the more an exercise is worked with, the more facility the group will demonstrate and the greater the benefit will be. The leader, however, needs to monitor the extent to which the exercise continues to capture the interest and energy of the group. If interest lags, then move on to something else.

five

Building Teams That Last

One of the questions I'm asked most often is, "How do you keep people motivated and committed to a ministry?"

Foster Community

The primary way is by creating an environment that fosters community. People desire to serve in a church ministry because they want to connect in a significant way with other people. Yes, they want to serve God, but they want to do it in the context of community. This may not be the felt perception of some people, but once they find themselves within a strong community, that community will become a very significant part of their fulfillment in ministry.

When asked, the drama team members at Willow Creek readily say that the most meaningful part of their experience on the team is the community we enjoy together. They get the experience of regularly performing in front of thousands of people, many participate at numerous conferences, some get to travel and perform internationally, and while these are all exciting and meaningful, still the number one reason why people on the team continue to serve year after year is community. I know this is true for myself. What I value most, both from the drama team that I lead and with the programming staff team that I serve, are relationships.

Many years ago, I learned a lesson I'll never forget on the value of community. It was our team's first get-together after a Christmas break. Because of a power failure in the building, I had to abort my planned training session. We ended up sitting in a circle on the floor in a stairwell where there was one emergency light on. I had to improvise, so I asked a simple question, "What was the highlight of your Christmas?" Various people shared what was more informational than revealing. Because I still had time to fill, I asked, "How about the downside of Christmas for you this year?" Over the next hour and a half, a number of people shared some significant challenges with their families, their work, and their health. Risk-taking and vulnerability were evident. There were tears and a lot of sensitive questions and interaction. We

> **The number one reason why people continue to serve year after year is community.**

ended with a time of prayer for those who were struggling. It turned out to be a very meaningful evening, far more valuable than what I had planned. A very simple, spur-of-the-moment question became a catalyst for an amazing experience in community. At the end of the ministry season we looked back on the year together, and a highlight for many wasn't a particular performing experience, or some breakthrough in acting, or some significant growth in acting workshops. No, the highlight was that night we all sat on the floor and shared our lives. The highlight that captured our hearts was community. Almost every year since that time I have used those same two questions on our first team night after Christmas.

What does it mean, in an ongoing manner, to create an environment where community can grow? First, community needs to be high on the list of ministry values. It is all too easy to develop a "Sunday to Sunday" mentality, going from one sketch to the next, being about the ministry task, and yet not intentional enough about the relational dimension of our teams. We, as ministry leaders, must fiercely protect community time. At Willow Creek a sketch has to happen every week, but there is no regular measurement for whether or not community is being fostered. If we're not careful, we can get so busy doing drama that we neglect the very thing necessary to keep our teams committed and fulfilled. If we do not pay attention to community, we will not keep our team members for the long haul. It's that simple.

> If we do not pay attention to community, we will not keep our team members for the long haul. It's that simple.

Nancy Beach, programming director at Willow Creek, has been a great example to me. Under her leadership I have learned firsthand the value of community. Equal to the value she places on excellence is the value she places on community. Our ministry is very fast paced, with more and more exciting ministry opportunities added all the time, but Nancy makes sure we take the time to stay connected. She leads a small group of ministry leaders who make up the Leadership Team for the Programming Department. Our decision-making becomes an extension of our community. (This is the same model used by the Leadership Team of the church.) Nancy regularly schedules retreats—a time for us to get away and do some department business—but by far the largest agenda item is to go deeper into community. I believe the major reason why the core of our Programming Department has such longevity is due to Nancy's leadership in this area.

One thing I've learned from Nancy is that no matter how hectic it gets, it's important to take time for community. So, in addition to having community high on your list of values, make sure, on a regular basis, that community is the "agenda." Some leaders resist this because they're concerned about the extra time it takes. Indeed, this is how I felt in my first year at Willow Creek. But we need to remember that this is what our team members are looking for (even if they don't know it).

I have tried to make time for community by working it into the rhythm of what we do. We meet as a team every Tuesday night for an hour and a half. Generally we will spend two weeks in a row working on the craft of acting; the third week is spent in community. We work on a 2 to 1 ratio, two nights of training to one of community. The community experience for us is achieved through small groups. The team is divided into small groups, with each group numbering 4 to 7. After two small-group nights, or once about every seven weeks, we have a "community night" when the whole team meets together. During this time we attempt to get caught up on the challenges certain members of the team are going through, or everyone will talk briefly about how they're doing. Sometimes I will simply pose a question like, "What are you thanking God for these days?" and those who feel like it will share. We always close by praying together.

> **No matter how hectic it gets, it's important to take time for community.**

Before developing small groups, this is how we handled community time. However, as the drama team grew, we found it was becoming more and more difficult to stay connected. We simply did not have enough time for everyone to share, and our community was not growing deeper. If someone had a major challenge in their life, they might resist talking about it because there were so many others who wanted to speak. At one point, I even resorted to setting time limits on how long people could share so we could get through the whole group in an hour and a half. It became clear it wasn't working.

As a leader, it was becoming increasingly difficult for me to stay connected with and to care for twenty-some people. But when I first proposed the idea of dividing the team into small groups, I met with some resistance. Many on the team liked the idea of everyone meeting together, and some were less than positive about a small-group leader assuming some of the role I had been playing. But we decided to give small groups a try for a year and then assess how we felt. It soon became clear to everyone that small groups were the best way to achieve an authentic community experience for our team. Though we are always fine-tuning and rethinking how we approach small groups, we now are committed to them.

Every drama team member at Willow Creek is strongly encouraged to be a part of a drama team small group. If someone is in another small group, they can opt out of involvement in one of our groups. However, very few do. I'm grateful for that because I am very attracted to the idea of ministry developing out of community.

The small groups are led by drama team members who have demonstrated leadership skill and a shepherd's heart. They assume responsibility for shepherding their group members, and I or another team member assumes shepherding responsibility for the small group leaders. We've experimented with coed as well as strictly male and female groups. Presently we are doing the latter and believe, for now at least, they work best. There is no set curriculum; rather each leader and team decide what they would like to do. Some groups focus on a traditional Bible study, others a book, but for all groups a large component is simply to enter into each other's lives. It's possible to have a small-group Bible-study experience where no real community occurs. We're not interested in that kind of group. Our model is that of Paul to the church at Thessalonica. He speaks of imparting not just the Gospel but also his own life for the purpose of encouraging walks that are "worthy of God" (1 Thess. 2:8, 12).

To authentically enter into another's life implies that the other person feels "known." And the larger the group, the more difficult it is to truly know each other. Ultimately, however, the extent to which any person is truly known has to do with how much one chooses to reveal. And revelation is always a matter of safety. A key to making a community experience work has to do with creating, as much as one can, an atmosphere of safety. There are no shortcuts. A feeling of safety occurs through incremental steps where the response to what is revealed is always carefully measured by the one who shares. We can say, "I want this to be a safe environment," but safety, like trust, is earned. That's why it takes time. It doesn't happen overnight.

One of the most enjoyable aspects of group life is to witness the gradual growth of trust and to see people in the group take risks and become more vulnerable. When one person risks, it encourages someone else to do the same. And gradually, over time, the depth of community increases.

I recently led a small group that included a couple men who were new to the team. I had become concerned about one man, for he seemed distant. His body language was saying one thing, while he maintained he was doing fine. Then one night he opened up and talked honestly about his insecurity, his lack of self-esteem, and fear of failure. It was great to see the group surround this guy with genuine care. I know he left that night feeling loved, something he desperately needed. And over the next few weeks, there was meaningful follow-up by at least two members of the group concerning the issues shared. When genuineness and vulnerability are modeled in a group, it gradually infects the whole group.

A few seasons ago, at a small group's first meeting for the year, Donna Lagerquist, who is as sensitive a shepherd-leader as she is a writer, asked, "In what specific way can this group serve you this year?" After some hesitation, Maggie said, "Get to know my mother." The group was aware that Maggie had an invalid mother who was quite draining, a woman who placed many demands on her daughters. Maggie felt that if she were to be truly known by this group, the group members needed to know her mother and thereby understand some of what Maggie had to deal with. So on a Saturday morning in early December, Donna's group all met at Maggie's sister's home, where her mother lived, and made Christmas cookies together. Maggie's mom loved it, especially the young children who came with their mothers! And Maggie felt served and loved by her small group.

A Win-Win Situation

One of the great by-products of fostering community on a drama team is that it has a payoff in performance. No theatre professional would question this. That is why there is so much effort by various theatre companies to foster a sense of ensemble, why directors create exercises to develop trust among cast members. Serious theatre practitioners understand that vulnerability is important in a performer, or that the better one knows those who they are acting with the stronger the potential for a good performance. The values of trust and safety are as important to cultivating strong performances as they are to developing strong community. Therefore, it is especially sad when church drama directors don't have community high on their list of values.

> **One of the by-products of fostering community is the payoff in performance.**

When Maggie joined the Willow Creek drama team a few years ago, she demonstrated much potential, but she was very insecure and really struggled with low self-esteem. Maggie was a beat-up person trying to figure out her life. I well remember those first rehearsals with her. She was so hesitant and unsure of herself and needed so much encouragement, I even questioned the wisdom of asking her to join the team. But gradually, with each performance, she grew stronger and more confident. At the same time, Maggie was in the nurturing environment of a small group, where she felt accepted and truly cared for. When she was unlovely, she was still loved. When she misspoke, she experienced forgiveness.

Over the years it has been a thrill to see Maggie blossom. She has become a top-notch performer. I have literally witnessed firsthand her growth in confidence and her belief in herself. It's apparent in her performing these days. She attacks a role with confidence and trust. She creates characters that are warm, real, sometimes poignant, but always delightful. I believe a large reason why Maggie has grown so much as a performer is because she has grown as a person. And this has been primarily through the process of her small group and the drama team as a whole. Growth as a performer is frequently the result of growth in community.

More Than Small Groups

Because of the importance of community, we also schedule other activities for the drama team to foster that community. Every summer we have a picnic, which includes families. At Christmas we have a party with our spouses. We periodically sponsor theatre trips into Chicago to see a show together. Individual small groups will get together informally for dinner or a movie. Every year we also have a drama team retreat. This involves an overnight together, and a large part of the agenda is to celebrate and affirm each other. These experiences, along with our times of ministry together, have created deep bonds of friendship among members of the team. This has been deeply fulfilling for me as a team leader.

Over the years this bonding has been forged through the kinds of experiences that inevitably befall any group. We prayed one of our members through the Betty Ford Center after he confessed to having a secret problem with alcohol. We supported one of our women through her struggle with bulimia, which necessitated intensive therapy, causing her to miss most Tuesday nights for more than a year. Today she is one of our key leaders. Another one of our women was cared for during numerous psychiatric hospitalizations. Today she is whole and fulfilled in ministry. We've supported others through loss of jobs, midlife crises, infertility, serious health problems, and some other issues that, because of confidences, I'm not free to write about. But, without question, our most significant experiences in community have been wrought through significant loss.

John's Story

John, one of our long-standing team members, and his wife, Jane, were expecting their first baby. His wife went into labor on a Sunday morning, and he called me with the news. Later that same afternoon he called again, this time with tragic news. He said the doctor had just informed them that the baby was dead. While impossible to imagine, Jane still faced the daunting task of delivery.

My wife, Kathy, and I immediately went to the hospital. We embraced John and cried with him. Other than assuring him that they were in our prayers, we had no idea what else to do. When I talked with John on Tuesday morning, I suggested, if he felt up to it, that he come to our drama team meeting that night. He told me that he didn't know if he could do it, but that he'd think about it. I tried to gently encourage him, saying it would be meaningful for us if we could pray for him and his wife.

That evening, twenty minutes into our meeting time when we were processing John's loss together, the door opened and in walked John. Immediately, the whole team rose to meet and embrace him. Obviously, there were many tears, lots of grief. Just a week before we had sat in a circle listening to this man describe how excited he was to be a father. After a while, John sat down in a chair and the rest of us gathered around him on the floor.

I will never forget what happened in the next hour. John talked. He said that he felt he had to be at our team meeting because "this is where I belong." He then told us the story and, through many tears, expressed how agonizingly difficult the loss of the baby was. Members of the team asked questions—sensitive, beautiful questions—that arose out of knowing this man and knowing what he needed to share with us. "What did she look like?" John told us in amazing detail. "What did you name her?" Katie. "How big was she?" These questions recognized and embraced the existence of this child, a fact that was very important to John. And his team knew it. He told us that he and Jane were planning a funeral, and he was even bold enough to say,

"I'd like you all to come." And we did. When someone asked if there was something we could send in lieu of flowers, John, because he felt safe, could say, "No, we like flowers." And there were lots of flowers. Before John left that night, we all gathered closely around him, laid hands on him, and prayed.

You do not go through an experience like this without it changing you. We ministered in a very significant way to John that night and in the weeks that followed. And he ministered to us. He taught us something about how to grieve authentically. He modeled for us the importance of asking for what one needs. For a period of time we, as a team, were unified in our focus on John and Jane and on what they needed. And we were bonded together as brothers and sisters in Christ.

Randy's Story

Randy, another long-standing drama team member, and his wife, Terry, had struggled with infertility for many years. We frequently prayed for them and God chose to answer with the gift of Gracie, an Asian infant whom they adopted. Shortly after Gracie's arrival, the whole drama team surprised Randy and Terry by arriving at their home one evening and singing "Amazing Grace" in the driveway. We then went into their home laden with gifts and refreshments. Together we celebrated the arrival of our answer to prayer.

In early January 1997, when she was five years old, Gracie was killed in a car accident. A county truck with faulty brakes crossed several lanes of traffic and collided with the family car Terry was driving. Terry was seriously injured (though now is completely recovered) and Gracie's two-year-old sister, Zoe, was uninjured. It was a horrific accident. Suddenly this child whom we had fervently prayed for, whom we had grown to love, was gone.

My wife, Kathy, and I arrived at the hospital shortly after Randy. I remember walking into a room, and there was Randy holding Zoe, weeping, saying over and over, "Gracie is dead, Steve." Overwhelmed does not come close to describing what Kathy and I felt in that moment. The situation was made worse by the fact that Randy was not allowed to even see his wife due to her condition.

In the next couple of hours, as best we could, Kathy and I tried to support Randy. Then gradually, on that very snowy night, members of the drama team began to show up at the hospital. By 10:00 P.M. about a dozen teammates, some with spouses, had gathered together. In all my years of ministry, I have never been so proud of my team—and it had nothing to do with performance. No one suggested they come, they just showed up. With each friend that arrived there were embraces, and a flood of emotion from Randy. We eventually all gathered in a waiting room, sat Randy in the center, and, through many tears, prayed.

As soon as we finished, the door opened and in walked John, who five years earlier had lost his little girl. I will never forget the moment when Randy saw John—how they met, embraced, and wept in each other's arms. We all knew that no one in the room understood Randy's pain like John. Now, years after his own tragedy, John was able to minister to Randy. What an amazing picture of community that little waiting room in that hospital became on that wintry night in January.

Randy and Terry asked Mark and me to officiate at the memorial service for Gracie. It was important to them that we use it as an opportunity to present the Gospel because they knew many nonbelievers would be in attendance. This wasn't hard to do, since Gracie was a little girl who had asked many she met, "Do you know Jesus?" Another one of their requests was that the drama team sing "Amazing Grace." So, at one point in the service, we all gathered around Terry and Randy and, as best we could, we did just that.

While the team for many months supported and ministered to Randy and Terry, the two of them also deeply ministered to us. Their authentic grieving, coupled with their unshakable faith in Christ, was amazing. I have no more tangible evidence of God's promise to comfort and sustain than what I have experienced through Randy and Terry.

And their story has had impact far beyond our team. The promise of Romans 8:28, that God can bring good out of all things, is evident in this testimony written by a woman who was baptized at Willow Creek in June 1998:

I always felt alone. No matter what relationship I was in. No matter how many friends I had. I felt ALONE. I had an empty fear inside and was afraid I would never find anyone who would truly love me. Every relationship I was in I would push to be loved, then give reasons not to. I sabotaged what I wanted. Over and over again I would go through this cycle.

I spoke with a Christian friend who had struggled as I did. She told me she prayed to God daily. So, I started. Every night. . . . I cried out to God. I did this for weeks before another friend offered to take me to a service at Willow Creek. We both cried at this service we were so moved. It was the one just after a five-year-old girl named Grace was killed in an auto accident. I remember asking myself, "How could God allow a beautiful, loving child to die? Especially from a family that prayed so hard to adopt her, and who had loved her so much."

And then I found out that her parents trusted God. And even though this tragedy happened in their life, they still loved Him and believed in Him. I wanted that!! That was the kind of love I had been looking for! A few weeks later I started in a seeker small group. Once I understood about Jesus and understood what He did for ME, I chose to believe and open my heart to Him.

I remember the pastor telling the congregation, at that first service, a little bit about the girl Grace. How she would walk up to people and ask them if they believed in Jesus. And how she would be real concerned for them if they didn't.

Even in her death, that little girl brought someone to meet Christ. This was my first lesson on how God can use a tragedy this awful and make something positive out of it.

Now, I am no longer alone. Never again will I be alone. When I begin to feel loneliness, I remind myself that Jesus is with me, and the feeling goes away. That simple! I still struggle. And I'm learning about myself and who I am. But I see all the blessing in my life, and when I come across trials I know that my God is in my corner. I will make it through.

Today Randy and Terry are stronger in their faith than ever before and both are deeply grateful for the support and love they've received in countless ways from their brothers and sisters on the drama team. Randy's passion for ministry has never been stronger, and this has been fueled in no small way by the care he's received.

If people are together in ministry over a period of years, they will inevitably experience losses and tragedies like those of John and Randy. Thank God we can be Christ to each other during such times. And God can use experiences like these to bring depth to the community of a group.

Impart Value

Part of what one receives out of a good small-group experience is the feeling of value. But the bestowing of value on one's team needs to be owned by every ministry leader. The church is far too guilty of using and abusing its people—both laypeople and staff. If ministry is ever to approach what God intends, this needs to change!

It's so basic. Everybody wants and needs to feel appreciated. And yet far too often we're so busy about the task of ministry that we fail to adequately express appreciation to those who are ministering with us. And the person they need to hear it most from is their ministry leader. The problem is that over time people begin to wonder if their efforts are appreciated, or if what they're doing is making a difference. We too easily assume that "surely one knows they're valued. Look how often they're asked to serve." It's like the husband whose love is questioned by his wife. "How can you wonder if I love you?" he asks. To which she replies, simply, "I need to hear it."

How does a sense of value become the *felt* perception for members of a team? Through action. Through speech. Taking the time to say, "Thank you, I appreciate the great job you did." Or writing a note, making a phone call, or taking a team member to lunch, all done in an effort to make them feel genuinely valued. The key word is "genuine." I've known people whose expressions of value are offered less out of sincerity and more out of a desire to keep the team members loyal, or to get them to do what is wanted of them. Eventually, however, a team member will figure this out and feel used. It's easy for ministry leaders to "talk value"; the test is whether team members *feel* valued.

Another way in which value is imparted is through respect. A person who feels respected does not feel used. As ministry leaders we need to be very careful of "arm twisting," of laying on pressure or a "guilt trip" if someone, for example, cannot perform when we need them. Some leaders make it sound as if a team member is "letting God down" if they don't respond to a ministry need. There are also team members who feel guilty if they can't perform even if there is no pressure by the leader. These people assume for themselves that they're letting you and the ministry down. When we detect this happening, we must let these people "off the hook." In a sense we need to save them from their own guilt-ridden thinking.

> It's easy for ministry leaders to "talk value"; the test is whether team members *feel* valued.

Feeling valued does not happen without open communication. We need, for example, to be in communication with our team members about issues such as frequency of performance.

Some people, because of their particular situation in life, can perform frequently, while others cannot perform more than once every two months and still maintain a healthy life. From time to time, for any number of valid reasons, a team member may need an extended break, or sabbatical. A leader may desperately need the person who is asking for some time away, but it would be a mistake to try to talk them out of it if the leader feels the request is for valid reasons. More likely than not, the team member will return healthier and with renewed energy for ministry.

Granting such a request says to a team member that they are more important than the needs of the ministry. Many ministries, though it may not be stated as such, function with these two values reversed, i.e., the ministry is more important than the individual. That's why people end up feeling beat-up and ultimately drop out. When team members feel genuinely valued for who they are more than for what they do, they probably will stay in ministry for the long haul.

One of the biggest challenges for a drama team leader is helping team members who perform infrequently to feel valued. Because they are asked to perform only a few times a year, in secondary roles, these people probably feel less important. Again, communication is the key. These team members need to be asked how they are feeling about their ministry involvement. I fear too often we wait until they come to us with their frustration before we say anything. I know I have. Approaching them first, before they complain, is a statement of value even if we can't provide a solution for their frustration.

However, I find that a number of these team members are relatively content. While they would like to perform more often, they are pleased with the opportunities they do have, and they enjoy the relationships and community that the team provides. It's especially important for them to hear from the ministry leader that they, too, play an important role. They should get regular, specific feedback on how they've grown and what areas of their acting they need to continue to work at.

Not everyone has the potential to be a primary performer, nor does everyone have to be. You may have members who have plateaued in their acting but are contented and productively serving the team. No problem. They should continue to be on the team. However, a team member who has "plateaued," who shows little possibility of getting stronger, and is discontented by their lack of performing, should leave the team.

One of the downsides of a strong community is that it makes it more difficult for people who should leave the team to actually do it for that entails leaving a group of people whom they enjoy. Thus, they may need a nudge from the ministry leader. This is always very difficult. But if a person is not content and the ministry leader has little reason for encouragement, then departure from the team is for the best. These situations need to be approached with much sensitivity and love, with the goal being for a team member to transition off the team and still feel valued as a person.

The Spouse Factor

Over the years I've discovered the importance of making sure, as much as one can, that the spouse of a team member also feels valued and appreciated. The whole spouse dynamic can be a challenging one. Here's a typical scenario:

A man finds himself on the drama team. He soon discovers not only a fulfilling ministry but also a community of people he enjoys and with whom he is developing friendships. His involvement takes him out of the home one night a week, and, in our case, for a good portion of Saturday and Sunday when he performs. Meanwhile his wife has to manage the children and the household alone. She's happy to do this, but it would be very easy for her to feel taken advantage of by her spouse and the church. If she is not involved in a fulfilling ministry, a subtle jealousy can creep in. She could even end up resenting her husband and the church that takes him away.

What can you do? First, be aware of the tension and the fact that some tension will exist no matter what the leader does. A leader should attempt to know the spouses and to specifically ask them periodically how they are doing. Ask as if you know it is challenging so that they feel the freedom to be honest. Simply expressing understanding and gratitude to the spouse goes a long way in helping the situation. But if you detect a major source of tension, this should be talked through with the team member and the spouse. Perhaps it's simply a matter of too much performing, which could be cut back. Or maybe the team member should take a sabbatical and focus on family for a while.

I also make it very clear to my team that when they say "yes" to a role, it means that it is not just okay with them but it's also okay with their spouse. I always respect a "no" when it is for family reasons or for a family commitment. Some team members have to be reminded periodically to check with their spouse before they say "yes." Sometimes a spouse will feel like a grinch if they're the major reason a team member cannot take a part. When that happens, the leader needs to make a special effort to support the spouse. Navigating this issue can be challenging, but it must be done both as a statement of value to the spouse and to maintain the team member's healthy participation on the team.

Another challenge for spouses, as well as for members of the church, is an issue of what sometimes is required during a performance. The question I'm asked most frequently centers on the issue of actors who are not married in real life playing a couple on stage. A sketch may require that actors touch, embrace, or, on occasion, even kiss.

Fueling the concern is what happens in Hollywood. How often have we heard about actors who have an on-screen romance and end up together in real life? Even though the problem isn't what happens in the movie—it's what goes on off screen—many jump to the conclusion that there is something inherently dangerous about two actors being "physical" during a performance.

Since it isn't realistic to rely only on married couples to play married people on stage, what does one do? First, underscore the fact that acting is just that, acting. Actors frequently are called upon to play people unlike themselves—unsavory, even evil characters. The idea that these characters, or situations, will some-how "rub off" on and influence the real behavior of an individual is, in the vast majority of cases, simply not true.

Part of the concern is due to a lack of understanding of the nature of acting. One does not really "become the character," even though it may appear that way. When two actors interact as though they are married, their performances are carefully coached. The embrace is always done the same way and under the watchful eye of a director. The actors are not encouraged to go off to practice their scene in a dark room!

Furthermore, an actor, while appearing in the moment, is also concentrating on his next line, or on an upcoming movement she wants to execute correctly. Actors are attuned to the audience and its reaction—or lack of it. In short, actors' minds are filled with the "business" of acting and not on how attracted they are to a member of the opposite sex with whom they are performing.

That being said, we can't be so naive as to assume this is never a problem. There are some people who are rather malleable psychologically and for whom this issue could be a stumbling block. Then these people should not be acting. If real feelings are always connected to action, if the distinction between real and make-believe is hard to maintain, then an individual should not act. Very few people, however, fall into this category. Even so, directors need to be attentive to the potential, albeit rare, problem that can emerge from doing scenes involving close physical contact.

When such a scene is necessary, I cast carefully, making sure, as much as I can, that the actors cannot only pull the scene off naturally but also are comfortable doing it. In addition, I frequently check in with spouses to make sure they're okay with what is done in a sketch. When I do encounter a spouse who is bothered by the issue, we talk it through. If he/she still is concerned, then I avoid using their spouse in a part which necessitates close physical contact with a member of the opposite sex. Periodically an actor is uncomfortable, for a number of reasons, in this kind of role. I respect that and do not force the issue.

There are many other parts that such an actor could play. In 99 percent of the cases, the best safeguard against this becoming a problem is working in community. The more that men and women get to know each other, the more comfortable they are with each other as brothers and sisters, the less likely the "touch thing" will become a concern.

Create an Atmosphere of Enjoyment

Obviously, a key ingredient in ministry fulfillment is enjoyment. Simply put, team members need to enjoy what they are doing. One of the main reasons people drop out of ministry is because they don't like what they're called upon to do. If someone is gifted in drama, there is a strong likelihood that person would enjoy being part of a drama team. That's why assessing a person's giftedness must come before a decision is made on where one serves.

Enjoyment, however, isn't automatic even if one has drama talent. Much has to do with how the experience is crafted by the leader. Is there confidence in the leader? Are rehearsals enjoyable? Are training sessions, in addition to being beneficial, fun? Or do they seem haphazard, with little apparent planning, and therefore of minimal value? Are sketches well-rehearsed and therefore enjoyable to perform rather than terrifying? (Due to the nature of performing, there will often be a degree of fear, some of which can be healthy. Inadequate rehearsal, however, leads to a damaging kind of fear.)

Provide Adequate Challenge

A fourth means by which to keep a team content in ministry is to provide adequate challenge, a factor that also increases enjoyment. Creative people need challenge; they will easily grow bored. A leader must stay one step ahead, always assessing what individual team members need in terms of training and performance challenge.

Like most directors, I try to cast actors in the kind of role that is their forte. Some are very gifted in the area of broad comedy.

Others can convincingly play a role that calls for significant emotion. Understanding areas of performance strength and casting accordingly is important in creating a strong team. However, always casting according to type can be frustrating for a team member, causing him/her to feel "boxed in" and underchallenged. As directors we need to take some qualified risks and cast to allow for growth.

This is harder than one would think. When excellence is our goal, the tendency is to cast the one person we think will be the absolute best in a particular role—the person who has been successful in this kind of part in the past. But it's likely that someone else on the team needs to be stretched. Thus directors must periodically be willing to take a risk. The resulting performance may not be as strong as it would have been if the veteran played the part, but providing a challenge and an opportunity for growth can be of great benefit to the actor who usually doesn't get to play such parts.

Sometimes we learn the hard way. I recently needed an actor to play an older, retired man of about seventy. This is a challenge since the oldest male on my team is under fifty. I do have a couple of actors who can do such roles quite convincingly, and they're the ones I rely on. However, for this particular week these guys weren't available. So I had to use another actor, who is very strong, but he's a young-looking thirty-six! Well, he ended up doing a great job, presenting a character of warmth and humor that was truly memorable. Sadly, I never would have cast him if it hadn't been for the fact that the "regulars" for this kind of part couldn't do it. And this actor would have missed a challenging and ultimately very fulfilling experience.

Periodically it's good to stretch the whole team. We've done a variety of performances with that in mind. A few years ago we presented excerpts from secular plays for an audience of staff and spouses. We also performed a full-length play, *Who Killed Richard Corey?* by A. R. Guney Jr. This experience was open to anyone on the team who wanted to participate. The same was true for a Christmas production we did called *When Angels Speak,* written by Sharon Sherbondy. Until *Richard Corey,* many on my team had never been in a play, only in sketches. We also have united three times with the music department to produce our own Easter musical drama, *The Choice*. (The publisher Word, Inc., has a musical of the same name.)

Because nearly everyone is involved, such experiences are good community builders for the whole team. They also inevitably produce artistic growth through a new challenge.

Churches, understandably, are limited in how many of these special projects they can undertake, if they can do any, because regular drama needs continue, week after week, month after month. But my hope is that at Willow Creek, in the future, we can do more small-scale production work of good secular material—plays that are about significant issues, plays that provide characters that actors can dig into. There is no better actor training than playing a challenging role.

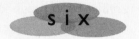

six

Writing a Winning Sketch

The presentation of quality church drama is contingent upon good scripts. Good acting and directing cannot save a script that is fundamentally poor. If church drama is to flourish, we need writers who understand playwrighting and know how to craft good drama. The dearth of quality drama for the church indicates that we have our work cut out for us.

What makes one script a winner and another a dud? The further they are from each other on a continuum, the easier it is to discern the difference. However, figuring out the difference between a 10 script (the best) and an 8 script is much more challenging. In this chapter I hope to clearly delineate the difference between strong scripts and weak ones but, more importantly perhaps, we can make some progress in understanding what separates an 8 from a 10.

At the outset it needs to be said that writing a good sketch is not easy, in fact it is deceptively difficult. This in itself helps explain why we don't have more good material. It isn't easy coming up with an idea that is engaging, creates high identification, and isn't predictable. It is hard to tell a story and create character through dialogue. It's difficult to hold the attention of an audience, let alone move them to laughter or tears. And we have to work within limits: a brief amount of time (at Willow Creek the rule of thumb is generally not to exceed eight minutes), and we write to set up a topic chosen by the pastor. We may not feel particularly inspired to develop a sketch that sets up a message entitled "Jesus, the Only Way to God," but that's what we may have to do. In some ways, one could argue, the limits help the creative process because it narrows the field. For the most part I think this is true, but it doesn't always feel that way, especially when one stares at a blank sheet of paper contemplating an assigned topic for far too long.

Before launching into the elements of a winning sketch, let me offer some advice to novice writers: write from your experience; write what you know. While that may seem basic, far too many beginning writers venture outside their knowledge or experience and write about what they think might be the case. When this happens, a script ends up sounding inauthentic; it appears less real. When given a topic, a writer needs to personalize it by finding ways to relate the subject matter to his own experience. On this issue noted author Ken Gire quotes from the film version of Louisa May Alcott's *Little Women*. When the title character Jo went to New York in an attempt to become a serious writer, she wrote stories she thought would sell rather than ones she felt passionate about. A new friend of hers, once a professor of literature, offers sage advice:

> "You must write about what you know, about what is important to you. . . . you should be writing something from your life, from the depths of your soul. There is more to you than this," he said, pointing to (her) newspaper story, "if you have the courage to write it."[1]

When writing is personal, it is courageous. We put it on paper and eventually on stage for "the whole world to see." But if we're willing to take this kind of risk, to be vulnerable, we have the potential to write not only scripts that will ring true, but ones that can wield real impact on an audience—an audience made up of many people just like us.

The Elements of a Successful Sketch

Conflict

The essence of drama is conflict. Conflict is what gives drama its drive, its energy. For the most part, the stronger the conflict, the better the script. Sometimes I read a script and it appears somewhat flat. The dialogue may be real, the characters clearly drawn, but it doesn't sustain interest. Frequently what's lacking is conflict. In its place we have characters "sitting around talking," but no one is at odds with anyone, no one is holding a position with which another disagrees. When this happens, drama is seldom compelling.

A beginning writer is well served by starting with two characters who hold opposite positions on an issue. This, along with stakes that are high,

> If we're willing to be vulnerable, we have the potential to write scripts that can wield real impact.

can produce some "fireworks" which can have the makings of good drama. Let's assume two characters, a husband and a wife. The husband has a new job opportunity that means relocating to another part of the country. He sees this as not only a professional advancement but also as a means to provide more for his family. His wife, on the other hand, is concerned about leaving extended family and pulling teenage children away from friends and out of a school they enjoy. Both are concerned about the stakes, which are high—the quality of their lives and the lives of their children. However, they strongly differ on the criteria. One values the opportunities afforded by more resources, the other values relationships. One has an entrepreneurial spirit and a thirst for adventure, the other doesn't want to disrupt the "apple cart" and is uncomfortable with change. Obviously, these differences can lead to some lively dialogue as this couple grapples with making a decision. Such a conflict will produce dramatic energy that has the potential to be captivating.

I believe the best sketches are the ones with the strongest conflict. That being said, it is also possible for a sketch to work even if it is not driven by conflict. This is true of one of our most

> **The stronger the conflict, the better the script.**

popular sketches, *Pulpit Talk*, which takes a humorous look at different preaching styles, ranging from the "terminator sermon" to the "feel good sermon." Though having no real conflict, the sketch is very entertaining and creates high identification. While extremely exaggerated, the sermons in the sketch are the kind that most everyone has experienced. And this underscores a general rule of thumb: if conflict is lacking, one needs to make sure something else will make up for it. In the case of *Pulpit Talk,* it is humor and high identification. No one notices the lack of conflict. But to venture away from conflict-supported drama is risky. Successful exceptions to the rule are rare.

Sometimes the conflict is internal, a struggle within a character, as opposed to between characters. Another one of our sketches, the previously cited *Nice Guy,* illustrates this kind of conflict. In this script a man basically listens to his friend's confession of something that happened years earlier. But there is no conflict between the two characters. However, the struggle within the central character, as he faces his failure and wrestles with guilt, makes the sketch work. Another factor that makes the script work is a pervasive sense of mystery as the story is gradually revealed.

Another one of our scripts, *Attractive Deal* by Mark Demel, is filled with tension, though it is not due to conflict between characters or even within them. Two coworkers find themselves together in the office late at night. The man has just closed a lucrative business deal, one which his administrative assistant has helped to win. As the two celebrate their victory, it becomes apparent that they are attracted to each other. They are interrupted by a cleaning person with a question. As the administrative assistant exits to attend to the issue, the man goes through his messages, sits down, and phones his father-in-law. In the conversation (we hear only one side) it becomes clear that the man is married, that his family is staying with his in-laws for the night, and that he and his wife are experiencing some difficulties. When his coworker returns, the nature of their interaction is such that, for the most part, we assume they will enter into an adulterous relationship.

In this sketch, there is no conflict between the characters, and not much internal conflict. The man and the woman are not wrestling with what they're tempted to do (though there is a little internal conflict created by the risk involved in being honest with each other). Yet, the "tension quotient" the audience experiences is strong. At first they wonder about the nature of the relationship and then where it is headed. As the two gradually give in to temptation, venturing toward a choice that will forever change their lives, tension is created by the question that looms for the audience, "Is this going where I think it is?"

Real

If drama is to have impact, it must be real, both in content and in how that content is communicated through dialogue. The issue of content has been covered in chapter 2 (see pages 27–31). But how does one go about creating dialogue that is real? One of our veteran Willow Creek writers, Judson Poling, says that we need to "let our ears do the writing." In other words, we need to listen to how people communicate and essentially write what we hear. Novice writers oftentimes write lines that are too long. Generally people don't speak in paragraphs. Dialogue, for the most part, consists of shorter lines, spoken "back and forth." The challenge is to present the story through the give and take of dialogue. In real dialogue, sometimes lines are left incomplete, or one person is cut off by the response of another. Writers must become students of dialogue. When in social gatherings, listen to and study the way people interact. The best school for dialogue happens every day, all around us.

According to poet and critic Samuel Coleridge, an interesting thing happens in the theatre. He calls it "a willing suspension of disbelief." While an audience knows a play or movie is not real, they choose to enter into it, to willingly suspend disbelief, to accept it as real. Some plays and movies, however, really challenge the ability to do this. For example, the current trend of action films, often bordering on the ridiculous, seriously strain credibility—even for an audience that wants to grant belief. How many times have you heard a response to a film such as, "I just couldn't buy it." Stilted and forced dialogue, or dialogue that seems contrived to make a point, also seriously challenges an audience's innate desire to believe what they see and hear on stage.

Broad and exaggerated sketches, ones which on the surface do not appear "real," can also work as long as they are rooted in true-to-life experience. One of the broadest sketches we have is *A Problem of Perspective,* by Judson Poling. A simple conflict between a husband and wife is played out three times, once as it happened and then from the perspective of the wife and then the husband. While the style is broad and humorous, the sketch is rooted in a recognizable truth: the tendency we all have, when there is conflict, to view our own perspective in the most favorable light. When sparks fly, we lose objectivity. When conflict happens, most of us have a hard time admitting we are wrong and tend to think the problem is more the other person's fault. Another sketch, Poling's *Early One Morning Just After the Dawn of History As We Know It,* presents two cavemen, who speak only gibberish, involved in a classic "keeping up with the Joneses" scenario. It begins with one caveman finding a rock to sit on instead of sitting on the ground. The other finds a bigger rock. Fueled by a competitive spirit, the first caveman pulls out a camp stool. The other responds with a chaise lounge. And eventually

> **If drama is to have impact, it must be real.**

a La-Z-Boy rocker ends up on stage. Ridiculous? Yes. Is it rooted in truth? Yes—in the temptation of materialism, the desire to have at least as much as, and preferably more than, our neighbors.

Audience Identification

The primary reason why being real is so important is that it aids audience identification. Drama does not work unless people can identify with it, unless it is apparent how what they see and hear relates to them. Good drama mirrors our lives, truthfully reflecting our experiences. A major reason why we are committed to doing contemporary drama at Willow Creek is because it presents people like you and me, dealing with real problems.

Good drama provides a vicarious experience for an audience. In short, through identification, an audience experiences what the characters do on stage. Without literally having the experience, through our God-given ability to imagine, we have it. This is the power of drama. Unfortunately, too often, especially in church drama, it's a power that goes unrealized. Characters who lack dimension, don't talk like "real" people, or seem contrived to make a point, all impede an audience's innate desire to believe. Too often we literally make it impossible for an audience to identify. When this happens, drama has lost its reason for being.

> **Unless people can identify with it, drama does not work.**

This is why it is so crucial when brainstorming sketch ideas to keep foremost in mind: relatability. One needs to ask, which of all these possible ideas will relate most directly to our audience? If your intended audience is made up of seekers, avoid developing an idea that would have stronger resonance with believers. It is easy to get caught up in an idea that is clever, or one that has potentially strong conflict, and forget the bottom-line issue: Will our audience identify with these characters?

Humorous or Moving?

Sometimes when I am reading a proposed script, the comments I hear from our programming staff are, "It's interesting, but I wish it was funnier," or "It doesn't really move me." I must admit, as correct as they might be, I don't like to hear comments like that because it means the writer and I probably have more work to do. The truth of the matter is that the more humorous or moving a script is, the better it will be. If it falls short of its potential to touch people deeply, or create peals of laughter, it might still work, but it might also be a bit more "flat" than the ideal.

Writing drama that is truly funny, or drama that moves people emotionally, is very difficult. In place of that which is genuine and honest, sometimes a script seems manipulated, or pushed, in an attempt to manufacture an emotional response. Or a script may have "laugh lines" that seem like that's what they are rather than lines which are funny but arise naturally out of character.

As hard as it is, thankfully we have the advantage of writing for audiences that want to laugh, and while they may not necessarily want to be moved, for the most part, people are open to being touched on an emotional level. This is why we go to movies. The point is, we don't have to sell audiences on the value of these kinds of responses; they intuitively respond. Half the battle is won. As writers, we just have to figure out how to genuinely enable the response.

Evident Structure

At face value, a script seems like a series of lines that tell a story. But in order for the story to be told well, it has to be supported by a structure. In the nineteenth century a Frenchman, Eugene Scribe, developed what amounted to a formula for playwrighting. While producing no plays of note, his more structured approach to playwrighting influenced later successful realistic writers, like Henrik Ibsen, and continues to influence writing today. While dangerous to speak of formulas when it comes to art, some of what these early realistic writers discovered can serve us in the task of sketch-writing today. The elements they found necessary to good play structure were:

- exposition
- inciting action
- rising action
- climax
- falling-off action

I believe these elements are generally found in the best sketches. The *exposition* is the background information we need to know in order to understand who the characters are as well as the nature of the problem or conflict. It's important to keep the exposition brief and to make it as interesting as possible. One of the biggest challenges with exposition is that it oftentimes sounds like the setup (which it is), rather than like good drama. Sometimes the way in which a line is said can help make it seem less expositional. For example, in a recent sketch it needed to be clear that a group of women donating their time to an inner-city medical center were work colleagues. When the women arrive, the character who organized the group says, "This is the center I've been talking about all week at work." That sounds like exposition. But by emphasizing "all week," as though saying, "That's about all I've talked about," the line sounds less expositional.

The *inciting action* is the introduction of the conflict. Once adequate background information is given, the real drama can begin. The *rising action* is the playing out of that conflict, which often rises, levels off some, and rises some more until the *climax,* or the emotional peak, is reached.

The *falling-off action* (denouement) is the "wrap-up," or the bringing of the action to a close. Sometimes this is referred to as the "resolution," but that term may imply that the problem is resolved. As has been said previously, this oftentimes is not the case.

Keeping these elements in mind can be very helpful to a writer as he structures a sketch, and an understanding of them is crucially important to the director and actors as they bring a sketch to life on stage (see "Staging a Sketch," page 151).

The following sketch, *Great Expectations,* by Sharon Sherbondy, is included to illustrate how the above elements function in a script.

(Setting: Two women, Kathy and Deb, sitting on a living room couch. Kathy is opening a gift.)

Kathy: Oh Deb, our first gift. This is so nice of you.

Deb: Hey, it's the least I can do.

Kathy: (holding up a Chicago Bears oufit for a baby) Oh, look at this. It's adorable.

Deb: I fell in love with it the moment I saw it.

Kathy: Can you believe that anything is this small? I just hope I know what to do with it once I get it.

Deb: It?

Kathy: I mean him. Him! Oh, Deb, I can hardly believe this is happening!

Deb: You've waited a long time for this.

Kathy: It seems like a lifetime. Now after all we've been through, our prayers are finally answered.

Deb: If it had been me I would have given up a long time ago.

Kathy: Listen, there were plenty of low moments, plenty of doubts. But I just had to force myself to keep thinking "someday..."

Deb: And that "someday" is here. Oh, Kath, I'm so happy for you. Not just because you're getting a baby but because you won't have to see any more agencies or doctors.

Kathy: (jokingly) It's a good thing because there's certainly nothing left of this body that hasn't been poked, probed, and stared at by at least a hundred people. After a while I quit asking their name and just said, "Take me, I'm yours."

Deb: And then, finally, you get the call.

Kathy: I couldn't believe it; I was in shock. I stayed awake all night just to make sure it wasn't a dream. And it's not; it's real. I just can't believe it.

Deb: How can that husband of yours work, knowing that in less than three hours he's going to be a father?

Kathy: I don't know, but I'm glad he's there and not here. We would have driven each other crazy.

Deb: Do you have a name for him?

Kathy: Uh, huh. Jason. Jason Carter.

Deb: Oh, I like that. Jason Carter. It sounds strong.

Kathy: I think so, too.

Greg: (entering, forced smile) Hi, everybody.

This first page of dialogue comprises the EXPOSITION. It includes all the information that we need to know in order for the real action to begin. The convention of a friend delivering a baby gift provides a realistic motivation for the two women to recount the challenge of the last number of years, but energy is also evident in the excitement of both women. This helps propel the exposition and keep it interesting. It also helps set off the REVERSAL, which will soon occur.

Kathy: Oh, hi, honey. I mean, "Daddy." Couldn't stay at work, huh?

Greg: No.

Deb: Congratulations, Greg. I can't tell you how happy I am for you!

Kathy: (showing him the outfit) Greg, look what Deb brought for little Jason. Isn't it cute? Our own little Chicago Bear.

Greg: Yeah, uhm, listen, Deb, if you don't mind, I'd like to talk with Kathy about something.

Deb: Oh, sure. I need to get home anyway.

Kathy: I think I've got a nervous father on my hands. What do you think?

Deb: I think you're right. (hugging them) Oh, I'm so happy for you two.

Kathy: Thanks, Deb. I'll see you tomorrow.

Deb: You better believe it. (she exits)

Kathy: Bye. Isn't she a good friend?

This section of dialogue creates some tension, for the audience begins to realize that some bad news is imminent. It also underscores Kathy's total preoccupation with and delight in what she thinks is about to happen. Greg is doing a good job of pretending, and neither woman picks up on any hints.

Greg: Yeah, she's pretty special. Uh, honey, I want you to come sit down. I need to talk to you about something.

Kathy: (lightly) Oh, my. This sounds serious.

Greg: Kath, it's about the baby.

Kathy: (still lightly) Greg, I already know what you're going to say.

Greg: I don't think you do.

Kathy: Look, I know ever since we got the call I've been thinking too much about the baby, but, honey, that will change. I promise I'm not going to become one of those mothers whose life revolves around her kid. It's just that right now it's all I can think about. I'm just so excited to see our dream finally come true.

Greg: Kathy, our lawyer called me at work a little while ago. The girl decided to keep the baby.

This line is the INCITING ACTION. It is the bombshell from which things begin to escalate.

Kathy: (shocked) What?

Greg: She changed her mind.

Kathy: But she can't do that! She signed the papers!

Greg: She has three days after the birth to change her mind.

Kathy: But she can't do that. She promised.

Greg: Kathy, she can do it and she did. Now, you knew this was a possibility.

Kathy: Where's Taylor's number? A lawyer should be able to do something.

Greg: I asked him and there's nothing he can do.

Kathy: What do you mean, you asked? You couldn't have or he'd be doing something.

These short, quick lines, as Kathy tries to reconcile to the reality, begin the RISING ACTION.

Greg: There's nothing he can do. It's already been done. Now please. (he goes to her, she pulls away)

Kathy: I don't believe you. It was all worked out. We had a baby. In just three hours he would be ours. He is ours.

Greg: (trying to console her) There'll be other babies.

Kathy: Other babies? I don't want other babies. I want this one.

Greg: Well, we can't have him, honey.

While both Kathy and Greg are feeling pain, the RISING ACTION is fueled by the tension between them. He, having had longer to process the information, is accepting it. She, on the other hand, still can't believe it.

Kathy: (pause) I can't take this anymore. What does he want from us?

Greg: Who?

Kathy: God, that's who.

Greg: Honey, I don't think this is His fault.

Kathy: Well, whose fault is it, then? He's the one I've been praying to for nine years asking for a child. But does He give me one? No. My body remains sterile and all the agencies just keep saying, "We don't have anything for you." And now this. Dangling this carrot in front of my nose only to yank it away. Well I can't take it anymore.

Greg: (crossing to her) Honey.

Kathy: (pulling away) Leave me alone.

As the RISING ACTION is played, it's important to find different levels. This section of dialogue provides that. The first line could be said more softly, as though defeated. On the "Whose fault is it?" line her frustration begins to grow until reaching a mini-climax with "Leave me alone."

(a pause. Greg crosses to the couch and starts to put the baby outfit back in the box)

This pause is key. The build to "leave me alone," followed by a sustained pause, helps set in relief the final build in the RISING ACTION to the CLIMAX.

Kathy: What are you doing?
Greg: I'm putting this away. We've got to take it back.
Kathy: How can you think about taking it back now?
Greg: Kathy, what do you want me to think about?
Kathy: Our baby!
Greg: Honey, we don't have a baby!
Kathy: Shut up! Just shut up! I don't want to hear it. I'm tired of hearing it.
Greg: (again going to her) Honey, please, just calm down. (grabbing on to her)
Kathy: (struggling to get free) I don't want to calm down. I'm angry. I hate that girl! I hate you! I hate me! I hate God! I hate this! I hate this. (breaks down crying in Greg's arms)

Obviously, this is the CLIMAX, the emotional peak. It's important for this portion of dialogue to be modulated so that it doesn't peak before the end of the section.

Greg: (long pause) Come on. Let's sit down. (they cross to the couch and sit)
Kathy: Oh, Greg. Where have our prayers been going? Why isn't God listening? Is there some sin in our lives? Are we doing something wrong? How long do we have to keep praying?

Greg: (simply, somewhat defeated as well) As long as it takes.

Kathy: But I don't have any faith left. I'm empty. Oh, Greg, what are we going to do?

Greg: I don't know, honey. (slowly) We'll just keep praying ... keep trying. (holding her close, tearful) We'll just keep trying.

LIGHTS SLOWLY FADE

This final section of dialogue comprises the FALLING-OFF ACTION, or DENOUEMENT. While not a resolution, it brings the action to a close.

Show, Don't Tell

One of the most basic principles of playwrighting is to show and not tell. The story has to be communicated in terms of action. Reminiscing or recounting something that has happened is never as interesting dramatically as seeing it played out. *Great Expectations* is a good example of this because we experience with the characters the confusion and tension created by bad news. They are not telling what happened; they are in the middle of it. The reason novice writers tend to tell too much instead of showing is that it is easier to tell than it is to communicate an idea through action.

For the sake of illustration, assume a scene involves two adult brothers who are in conflict because trust has been broken. A number of issues have led to the major breakdown, but the "straw that broke the camel's back" is that the younger sibling borrowed the other's car without asking and had an accident that caused major damage to the car. To talk about this issue in terms of "remember when" is much less interesting dramatically than to dramatize the point at which the older brother discovers what his sibling has done. This is immediate, the emotion is "in the moment" and not something recalled.

We recently did a sketch on the subject of power for a series entitled "Money, Sex and Power." *Power Trip,* by Sharon Sherbondy, is a great example of a sketch that shows rather than tells. A high-powered man arrives at an airport in a snowstorm for a business trip to Arizona. Frustrated by the number of people waiting at the ticket counter, he pretends to know some people in order to cut in line. When he gets to the counter, the ticket agent tells him his flight has been canceled. He tries every trick to get what he wants—he smooth talks, intimidates, pulls power plays—because, he shouts, "I don't get canceled!" He refuses to accept the fact that he cannot get what he wants. The word "power" is never used, but it clearly is this man's problem.

Sometimes when I read scripts by novice writers I have the feeling that the best drama is not even in the script but in what has come before (or even what comes after). Assume another scenario where a husband and wife are at odds over the manner in which one of them handled a situation involving their teenage daughter who was out far past her curfew. Rather than have this described as a past action, it would be better to show the parent dealing with the teenager while the other parent looks on. Perhaps, prior to the confrontation, the observing parent said, "You can handle it this time." After the teenager heads off to her room, the parents, now in the heat of the moment, can "go at it."

However, sometimes "telling" is necessary. Periodically a script comes along that breaks this "rule," yet still works. Our script *A Nice Guy*, which is primarily recollection, is still effective due largely to the dramatic nature of the story told. In fact the story, involving the vicious taunting of a child, is such that to see it played out would be difficult, perhaps even melodramatic. The impact of the memory on the storyteller also helps sustain dramatic interest.

Economy of Words

In all forms of playwrighting, economy is important. In other words, only what is absolutely necessary should be included in a script. One of the major pitfalls of sketch writing is the tendency to try to cover too much. The scope of a sketch needs to be limited. An eight-minute script cannot have a subplot; there is no time to develop it. One also has to be very careful about the number of characters; each character has to be thoroughly justified. A general rule of thumb to test scope is that you should be able to summarize a good sketch in one sentence.

In addition to a limited scope, a script should have no excess verbiage. A writer should be able to justify why each line is necessary, either for background information, to advance the plot, or for character development. If a line is not achieving one of these objectives, it should be cut. But this is easier said than done because sometimes a writer's favorite lines, the ones she labored most over to get them just right, are the ones that need to go. Judson Poling refers to this painful process as "all your darlings must die!"

> A script should have no excess verbiage. A writer should be able to justify why each line is necessary.

While that may be a bit dramatic, there is much truth in it.

An editor, working with a writer, can be very helpful in "pruning" a script. An editor brings an objective perspective to a writer's work. A writer gets so close to what she has written that oftentimes perspective is lost. She may think a line, or even a character, is necessary when it is not.

I realize that most writers do not have the advantage of working with a good editor. But sometimes this happens because we don't seek one out, because we fear that someone else will "rip my work apart." Holding on to what we've written, preferring not to have anyone else involved, is unfortunate and a detriment to the development of a good script.

A writer needs to realize that a good editor is an ally, one who is committed to making the script stronger. An effective editor does not run "roughshod" over a writer's work, but rather asks questions and suggests changes. An editor should, as much as possible, leave the rewriting to the writer, and on those occasions when an editor does rework a line, approval of the writer should be sought. Obviously, trust is important in making the whole process work. And trust is something that is earned over time and through experience.

How does one go about finding an editor or, at the very least, someone who can provide a fresh perspective? While uncovering such a person is not easy, perhaps there is someone in your church who, over time, has shown good instincts in terms of drama. Maybe it is someone on the acting team. Experiment a bit by asking a few individuals to give you feedback on a script. Eventually someone may emerge who can assist you. Also, networking with other writers in other churches can be a great means of support. Attending conferences by organizations such as Christians in the Theatre Arts (see Appendix) or the Willow Creek Arts Conference can help a writer contact other people who could provide perspective and assistance in developing strong scripts. Perhaps a kind of partnership can develop where two writers assist each other with their writing efforts. Above all, be open. Solicit input from others—actors, pastor, spouse, friends. Again, oftentimes we don't get feedback because we don't ask for it. Obviously, we're not obligated to take every suggestion we get, but someone might raise just the right question that results in an improved script.

In the interest of developing scripts that are tight and economical, it is important to have adequate time. Setting aside a script that you've worked on for a few days and then coming back to it can reveal much that needs to be changed. It never ceases to amaze me how one can work hard to get a script just right, only to return to it a while later and see much that isn't right! Revisiting our work after gaining some "distance" from it always produces better scripts.

Suspense and Surprise

If we guess the punch line of a joke before it is said, the joke isn't funny. If we figure out how a sketch will end before it is finished, the sketch will be less effective. Another principle we have learned from the "well-made play" structure and the realists of the nineteenth century is the importance of suspense, complications, and reversals.

Where is this going? is one of the questions that helps sustain the interest of an audience. Sometimes we're led to think one thing when another is happening. In our sketch *Reality Therapy* a number of such reversals occur. When a couple realize that a soon-to-be-married relative and her fiancé have never had a fight, they decide to rectify the situation. The couple plan a card game, which is sure to create some friction. However, during the card-playing, it is the married couple who get into a big fight. The embarrassed and shocked engaged couple sneak out. After the door closes, the married couple break into laughter, "high-fiving" each other over how good their performances were. While the audience thought one thing—that card-playing would spark the engaged couple's first argument—the married couple actually had faked a fight to scare some reality into the other couple. This twist is a surprise to the audience, a reversal both unexpected and entertaining. The sketch ends with yet another reversal when the couple begin to recount what each said in the "fabricated" argument. They each begin to take offense and the sketch ends with the couple in a virtual standoff.

A surprise ending also is evident in Donna Lagerquist's sketch *Love Is in the Air*. The setting is the cockpit of an airliner. Through the course of the action, the copilot and navigator end up thinking the pilot and flight attendant are planning to spend the layover in San Francisco together. At the end of the sketch, we discover that the pilot is planning an affair—but with his wife, who is a passenger on the plane. Endings such as this, that are different from what was expected, are very satisfying dramatically.

Safeguards to Developing Strong Scripts

Rewriting

Neil Simon's autobiography is appropriately titled *Rewrites*. As a playwright he has spent much of his life reworking what he has already written. It is sobering to read his account, especially his early attempts at writing, and the extensive amount of total rewriting of scripts that he did, sometimes even after a play opened! Anyone who wants to write needs to accept the fact of rewriting. On the amateur level, many resist this due to an "it's good enough" attitude. But often it's avoided simply because rewriting is too much work. At Willow Creek we've had many potential contributors come along who were interested in writing for us. I give them an assignment and then respond to their work, usually suggesting some changes. Generally, these novice writers hang in there for a while, but eventually 99 percent fade from view and are never heard from again. I fear most think their first efforts should end up on stage and, when this doesn't happen, they give up and stop working at it. But good writing is hard work and it takes time. Many potentially gifted writers stop trying too soon. I often wonder what sort of contribution these people could be making today if they had hung in there.

Thankfully, Donna Lagerquist, one of our writers, didn't give up. Donna has been an actress on Willow's drama team for about sixteen years. Approximately ten years ago she expressed an interest in writing and began giving me sample scripts. Her early sketches were long, unfocused, and often had too many ideas going, but I saw in them some real genius, some extraordinary creativity. While her early scripts had too many characters, some of those characters were very engaging. Over the years Donna committed to developing her gift, and this took hard work and tenacity. Today Donna is a prolific writer. Now when she gives me a script, it is most often focused and has no excess verbiage. It is developed around a creative idea and has interesting characters. Some of the most significant moments in services at Willow Creek have been the result of Donna's wonderful work. Thank God she stayed with it.

> **Anyone who wants to write needs to accept the fact of rewriting.**

Team Approach

One of the true delights of my job is watching a script develop from an idea, to a first draft, through rewrites, to a fully realized performance on stage. Throughout the process many people have a hand in shaping the script. I've already talked about the importance of an editor who works with the writer. At Willow Creek, before a script is scheduled for performance, it needs to be approved by the programming staff, who will often make suggestions to improve it. In rehearsal, further shaping happens when the actors work with the script. At this stage, lines are often cut, added, and changed. This all means that the writer of the script has to hold it loosely. Our writers have learned that this process makes their scripts stronger. But I've also known writers who are suspicious of such a group creative process, believing the script needs to be a "single voice." While consistency of character and "voice" is a valid concern, it can be achieved by asking the writer to make (or approve) a change that's suggested by a director or actors. A controlling writer, whose reflexive response to a request for a change is "That's not how I see it" curtails creative input from others who could help to make the script stronger. I love the fact that the writers I work with present their scripts as an offering that they know will invariably be adjusted in the approval and rehearsal process. And as long as the writers are pleased with what they see on stage, they will continue to support a team approach.

Time Line

At Willow Creek it generally takes about 3-1/2 weeks to develop a script from idea through performance. I'm not suggesting that this is the preferred amount of time, only that this is our time line. Generally, more time is always preferred, but since we do drama every week, this time line works for us. For those in the beginning stages of drama ministry, more time is crucial.

Three and a half weeks prior to a weekend we have a brainstorming meeting for that service. We try to have as much information as possible regarding the topic from the teaching pastor. The more information the better. In this meeting, made up primarily of programming staff members, we try to come up with song ideas as well as an approach for the sketch. Sometimes we end up with a rather developed drama idea that we all like; other times all we have are a few angles to explore; and periodically we come up dry. One of our writers is then approached. We give them the information we have with regard to the topic and share the ideas we have come up with. We always like to give the writer some possible directions to explore. Obviously, this is better than simply saying, "Here's the topic, now come up with something." The writer is always free to either develop one of our ideas or come up with something totally different. If we strongly prefer a particular idea, then we will communicate that and ask the writer, if possible, to take this approach. Though, again, the writer, if he/she cannot connect with the idea, is free to go in another direction. The writer then takes about a week and a half to develop a script. We take about another week to rewrite and fine-tune the script. Sometimes, if the initial script is not strong enough, we will start over on another idea. Our goal is to have a finished script in the actors' hands one week before the sketch will be performed.

Sketch Evaluation

The following checklist is intended as a guide, not a foolproof means of script evaluation. A good sketch does not necessarily include all these elements, but many should be evident. I hope this list can help you in assessing the merits of a particular script.

The sketch:

____has clear and adequate conflict

____if lacking conflict, what makes up for it (i.e., high identification, very moving, highly humorous, etc.)?

_____

_____

____exposition is handled concisely and clearly

____is clever

____is engaging and holds attention

____creates high audience identification

____has a single focus, does not cover too much

____is clear and concise; no "deadwood"

____is about a real issue, and is handled in a realistic manner

____characters are sympathetically and credibly drawn

____if broad in style, is *rooted* in reality

____dialogue sounds like real conversation

____"earns enough," in other words it would add to a service and merits the time necessary to perform

____shows rather than tells

____does not preach

____avoids pat answers to complex issues

____is touching or funny

____is not melodramatic

____the humor is not forced or extraneous to character or situation

____demonstrates a clear sense of suspense

____is not predictable

____clear structure (inciting action, rising action, climax, etc.)

seven

Effective Directing

I used to say, "Ninety percent of directing is common sense." I no longer say that. That's because I have seen too much drama in churches that indicates a lack of understanding the basic rudiments of directing. Thus, this chapter will offer practical tools and principles that can be used to craft effective drama. Over time, through experimentation, these tools can unlock the mystery that confronts novice directors—"What do I do with actors on a stage?" One of the most instructive ways to begin is by discussing what pitfalls to avoid. Much can be learned by simply understanding what good directing is not.

Directing Pitfalls

Slow Pace

I believe the number one inhibitor of effective drama is pacing that is too slow. At a drama conference a few years ago I had the rather difficult experience of seeing one of our better sketches performed by another group. It took almost twice as long in performance as it should have. It was agonizing. It not only fell flat, it died! The two actors had ability; the problem was largely a matter of pace. Lines were said too slowly, too methodically, and cues—the space between lines—were far too slow. I joke with my own actors, when a particular cue is slow, by saying, "You could park a semi-truck in that space." This pitfall is especially evident in amateur productions when one character asks another a question. For example, one says, "How about a movie tonight?" The other actor thinks and thinks and then thinks some more, finally responding with, "I don't think so. I'm too tired." But it is very clear that the length of time it took to process the simple question was far longer than it needed to be. There needs to be what I term "response time," but oftentimes a mere "beat" is all that is needed.

Pace often sets pros apart from amateurs. When drama is done well, it progresses faster than one would think. The next time you experience good drama, distance yourself from it a bit and observe how quickly it moves. You might be surprised.

Another factor in pacing is affected by the media. Information, whether in a sit-com or in a television commercial, comes at us in what is often a breakneck pace. This is what people are used to. It is no wonder, then, that a sketch performed at First Church, which moves along at a snail's pace, fails to keep the attention of its audience. I find it interesting that a popular television show like "Seinfeld" contains about twenty scenes in a twenty-two-minute episode. The average scene lasts about a minute then,

> **The number one inhibitor of effective drama is pacing that is too slow.**

suddenly, after some fast-paced music, we're at another place with different characters. Like it or not, such programming is a huge factor in determining the attention span of our typical audience member.

One caution about pace. Obviously the pace needs to be appropriate to the situation. Sometimes a slower, more reflective approach is necessary. At other times a long pause can be very effective. Pace is defined as "information flow." As long as information is being communicated, and the action is compelling, any pace can work.

Some directors would argue that just saying "pick up the pace" is insufficient. Far better to query the actors and discover why, for example, they're taking so long to ponder a question by another character. In this way the actor internalizes a reason, rooted in character, that determines the pace, rather than simply having it imposed by a director. While this approach has much merit, I believe it is still effective, and necessary, to say to your actors on occasion, "We've got to pick it up."

Low Energy

Often related to pace is a lack of performance energy. If the pace is too slow, generally the energy will be low as well. Energy can be a problem even if the pacing is fine. While energy, or a lack of it, is easy to discern, it is more challenging to define exactly what it is. Energy gives drama its charge, its drive, the sense that it is "going somewhere." While related to volume, it is much more than that. Performers who demonstrate energy are ones who appear connected to the parts they play. They act from the "gut" and thereby communicate that the stakes are high.

Energy is often innate. As I described in a previous chapter, it is one of those qualities directors look for in an audition. At times it's necessary to work with an actor to improve their energy output. A few years ago we added a man to our team who we knew needed work in this area. He had little previous drama experience, but was natural and believable in performance. His main problem was that he lacked energy. Getting this actor to a consistent, acceptable energy level has taken time. After three years, he still has a tendency to dip in energy, and he needs to be reminded to "speak louder," "stay connected." Sometimes it helps to dialogue with an actor: "How much does your character want this? Why? What will happen if you don't get it?" One of the dangers when working on energy is for an actor to begin pushing, at which point it seems forced and less real. In short, it can begin to appear "acted."

Actors like this need consistent feedback on when they are appropriately energized so they can begin to sense for themselves when they have it and when they don't. In acting, appropriate energy, along with a believable character, must be evident.

Poor Blocking

"Blocking" refers to the placement and movement of actors on a stage. Assisting actors in creating effective blocking is one of the most important contributions of the director. Many novice directors have little knowledge of how to achieve good blocking. The extent of some directors' directing amounts to saying to their actors, "Do whatever feels natural." This is of virtually no help to beginning actors, who by the mere fact that they're on a stage feel very unnatural. Immediately they become self-conscious and express concern over what to do with their arms and hands. We go through life without ever thinking of the appendages that hang at our sides, but the moment a beginning actor gets on stage, that's all he can think about.

> **Assisting actors in creating effective blocking is one of the director's most important contributions.**

It's not surprising that a beginning director tells actors to "do what's natural" because when drama is done well, it looks natural and real. In good drama the craft of the director should not be noticed. This "hidden craft" of the director causes many to assume the role of director without ever realizing that there are tools and principles that can be used to create effective blocking. When this happens the extent of one's directing amounts to little more than letting actors "run through it." More about this later.

One Dimensional

Good drama, if graphed, would have rises and falls as it gradually builds to an emotional peak. Effective drama is made up of a series of "builds"—sections of dialogue where the emotional energy rises—that lead to the climax. In a bad performance, there are no builds, rather the sketch just "sits there." If put on a graph, all you'd see would be a flat line. In an intensive care unit a flat line on a monitor indicates death. So too in drama. In a well-written sketch this "rise and fall" is evident in the text, but too many directors do not discover it or play it. Thus, it is paramount that actors, led by the director, understand the action of a sketch and make choices about which sections should build in energy or tension. The actors also must understand where the emotional climax is and make sure they don't "peak" before they get there. If this is not done, the performance will not be interesting or engaging.

Rhythmical Pattern

While patterns are nice in wallpaper, they are never good in drama because they lead to boredom. One way an undesirable pattern can sneak into a performance is through rhythm or cadence of speech. In drama there is a tendency to subconsciously imitate the pattern of speech of the actor one is playing opposite. If a director does not catch this, pretty soon the whole performance can fall into a kind of cadence which has a lulling effect on an audience. It's important that each actor discovers the appropriate rhythm of speech for their character, thus avoiding an unappealing pattern.

Appears "Acted"

When an actor seems to be acting, he is not real. Ideally we want actors who appear real. Just as some preachers have a tendency to put on a voice when they step behind a pulpit, some actors do the same thing when they assume a role on stage. And experienced/trained actors are not necessarily the answer. I have worked with many trained actors who "act" rather than appear real. One advantage of working with people who have little or no experience is that they have not developed bad habits. As I said previously, the number one thing I look for in an audition is naturalness. Without naturalness, drama does not work.

One sure way for acting to become too big and overblown is for actors to project, or act, for the people in the back of the theatre or church. I have been amazed by the number of amateur directors who encourage their actors to do this. If our facial expressions or mannerisms are "big" enough to register in the outer reaches of our space, then surely they will be far too big, even ludicrous, for people closer to the stage. And other actors are forced to play opposite broad caricatures rather than believable characters. Worst of all, actors are being taught to "act" as opposed to simply being real. Actors need to speak and react in ways that are real to the actors they play opposite on stage rather than for an audience member in the last row. While actors need to project vocally and be heard by people in the back row, they are developing bad habits if they try to "project" their faces that far.

Creating Movement

Before discussing specific tools for creating blocking, a couple of overarching blocking issues need to be considered. First, good blocking tells the story. If one were able to turn down the volume, so to speak, the basic conflict or tension should be seen in the movement. By simply watching the action, a sense of the essential story should be evident.

Second, good blocking uses the stage well and creates appealing stage pictures. The stage is a kind of palette with an aesthetic dimension. Visual interest is key. When the director as an artist in the theatre first arose in the late nineteenth century, much emphasis was placed on stage composition. Early directors, like the Duke of Saxe-Meiningen, were known for their beautiful composition of crowd scenes, which were like paintings. In a day and age when little thought was given such composed staging, the Duke's work was considered amazing. Modern directors would consider his work as over-composition and criticize it for drawing attention to the director. While today we have moved away from such over-composition in favor of something more natural, nevertheless good use of the stage and an aesthetically pleasing look are essential.

Third, in blocking, naturalness takes precedence over blocking rules. Another inheritance from earlier directors is a series of "rules" which can at times be useful but are now generally regarded as antiquated. These rules range from "Always kneel on your downstage knee," to "Always gesture with your upstage hand," to "Don't put your back to the audience." These rules were all about keeping an actor open to the audience as much as possible. While, for the most part, it is important to be open and visible to the audience, sometimes it works well to have an actor turned away or even have her back to the audience. Often it is more natural for an actor to use his downstage hand to gesture (especially if he is right-handed and standing stage right). Such a gesture may close the actor off a bit from the audience, but it may be more natural.

Fourth, blocking cannot be optimal for all members of the audience. If directors block so that their entire audience can see everything clearly, the movement will be flat and uninteresting. If one works in a space where the audience is curved around the stage, optimal staging for the people on the extreme sides is impossible. A rule of thumb is to block for the majority, and move actors often enough so no one's view is obscured for too long.

Six Tools for Effective Blocking

In the following, I have tried to reduce the basic essentials of creating movement to a few tools. I believe that an understanding of these principles, and experimenting with them, will, over time, vastly improve the beginning director's work. The list starts with some very basic principles, but ones which I include because they are too often not adhered to by the novice director.

1. Movement needs to be motivated

The most important principle of blocking is that all movement needs to be motivated. There must be a logical reason for every move. Some movement is called for in the script, i.e., the phone rings and an actor has to cross to pick it up, or there is a knock at the door and it needs to be answered. The motivation for this kind of movement is obvious. However, the vast majority of movement in drama is not called for in the script; rather it is movement resulting from the action of the drama. If, for example, a scene involves a confrontation between two characters, the movement would underscore the tension of the scene, perhaps culminating in a literal face-off center stage. In staging such a scene a director and actors have an unlimited number of choices, with each director's approach being different. There are many right choices, as long as there is clear motivation. If there is a reason for an actor to cross, sit, cross away, then the movement should appear natural. While the audience does not consciously judge the validity of all the movement, they just perceive that it makes sense.

In amateur drama productions, . . . it is not uncommon to see movement that defies reason.

This foundational principle is frequently broken in amateur drama productions, where it is not uncommon to see movement that defies reason. Often it is nervous actor movement, or movement the director has left up to actors to devise, actors who do not understand that each movement needs motivation. It is the director's job to safeguard this principle. Whether the move has been suggested by the director or assumed by an actor, it is the director, from her more objective position, who must closely monitor all of the movement.

2. Stand still, avoid shifting weight

This is another basic principle, but one which, again, is too often not evident in amateur drama. This is damaging because it draws attention to the actor, who oftentimes has simply not been told to stand still (as opposed to weight shifting which has been directed as part of character). So this nervous, novice actor, who does not feel very natural on a stage, ends up expressing physically the discomfort he is feeling inside. This is the same actor who worries about what to do with his hands, and in addition to shifting weight experiments with various distracting arm and hand positions. This problem is easily solved by a director simply saying "stand still." To which an inexperienced actor will say, "You mean it's okay to just stand here with my arms at my sides?" That realization is amazingly freeing for a new actor, who then needs consistent, genuine feedback from the director when he is doing well.

Actors need to be aware of the fact that movement draws focus. This means that, all other factors being equal, an audience member's eye will immediately go to what moves. So an audience supposed to be focusing on a touching speech by an actor standing center stage, but not moving, can easily have their attention drawn away by another actor who simply moves her arm or shifts weight.

> **Actors need to be aware of the fact that movement draws focus.**

In a recent Good Friday presentation at Willow Creek, this was an issue. We did a piece involving a corps of actors and three singers. The singers were on stage the whole time, woven throughout the drama portions of the service. During an important climactic speech by an actor standing still downstage center, one of the singers, positioned fairly far upstage, scratched an itchy nose! The attention of many in the audience immediately shifted from the actor to the nose scratcher. Knowing that it might be distracting, the singer even tried to move his hand slowly, but this only made it worse.

3. The "cross away" and "cross away and turn" technique

This technique is the most important one for creating effective movement. When understood, it unlocks literally unending movement options. (The technique is demonstrated in the CD-ROM included with this book.) Let's return to the confrontation scene between two actors. They are now in the midst of a heated discussion which has brought them, face-to-face, center stage. Now what? They cannot cross closer together. When this principle is not used, the actors end up being stuck center stage. Perhaps they back up a few steps and then come together again, but this is not very interesting. In order to open up more movement options, one actor, on his line, can simply cross away from the other. Let's assume that the line is, "I don't care what you say, I'm not going. And that's final!" It could be said while simply facing the other actor. Or, on the first part of the line, "I don't care what you say, I'm not going," the actor could turn and cross away from the other and then, for emphasis, turn back and face the other actor on "And that's final!" With distance between the actors, you have created some options. Perhaps now the other actor crosses to the first one on his line, "I knew it, you can't be trusted," only to have the first actor cross away in front of the other when he says, "This has nothing to do with trust." So, in essence you create a kind of cat and mouse, pursue and pursued, movement pattern (see the CD-ROM).

At first this crossing away from the person one is speaking to can be problematic for an actor who isn't used to it. When asked to try it, he will frequently cross away, but try to look back at the other actor while doing so. This ends up looking thoroughly strange, as though the body were going in two directions. The actor simply needs to be encouraged to turn and cross away and not look back, being careful to use his arms and body to motivate the cross. Another actor may turn and cross without looking back, but if his arms remain stiffly at his sides and his eyes seem focused on one spot, the move probably will not work. For the move to be effective, the actor must have more of a scattered eye focus and use his arms to help motivate the cross (see the CD-ROM). It takes some experimentation, but with careful observation and coaching by the director, naturalness can be achieved rather easily.

This kind of movement is an accepted convention of the stage, but it is also rooted in human experience. We don't always look at the person we're speaking to.

Let's go back to the original set of lines:

Actor 1: I don't care what you say, I'm not going. And that's final!

Actor 2: I knew it, you can't be trusted.

Actor 1: This has nothing to do with trust.

Using the same principle, we'll make different choices. Instead of crossing away on the first line, the actor could say the first part to the other and not cross away until "And that's final!" This time the actor chooses to stay facing away. His move away is motivated because it underscores the fact that he's not leaving. The other actor does not cross on "I knew it, you can't be trusted," but rather stays where he is. The other then turns back defensively and says, "This has nothing to do with trust."

Another option might be for Actor 1 not to cross on the first line, rather after he says, "I'm not going," Actor 2 crosses a few steps away in disgust, to which Actor 1 says, for emphasis, "And that's final." Actor 2 then turns on "I knew it, you can't be trusted," with Actor 1 crossing to the other on "This has nothing to do with trust." These few lines of dialogue can be staged numerous ways, using different blocking choices, which are demonstrated on the CD-ROM.

One of the keys in this technique is to use the turns for emphasis. One can see how lines like "And that's final," or "I knew it, you can't be trusted" can be underscored nicely when the turn back to face the other actor is coordinated with the line. It is easy to get sloppy. It's easy for actors to anticipate the move and turn a bit prior to the line. Then, instead of achieving natural character movement, the move just looks like assigned blocking. Again, it is the director's job to watch for this and remind the actor that the turn needs to be executed at the precise spot in order to underscore the line. This all may sound rather formalistic and a bit "picky," but it is with this kind of detail that effective, motivated stage movement is created. And your actors will like the detail. Such movement choices provide a clear foundation upon which an actor can add elements of characterization.

Such precise blocking provides the much needed security that especially novice actors need.

4. Breaking up lines with different blocking choices

This point is really a further elaboration of number three. As directors approach a script they need to assess each line, thinking in terms of meaning and interpretation. They then need to consider blocking choices which support the interpretation. It is oftentimes helpful to think of various choices for different parts of a line. Consider the line, "What are you talking about? That's the most ridiculous thing I've heard. Good luck!" It's possible, though not necessary, to ascribe three different moves to that one line. For example, on the first part of the line, "What are you talking about?" an actor could stand up. On "That's the most ridiculous thing I've heard" they could cross away, and then turn back on "Good luck!" In the director's goal of interpreting a text, the impact of simple crosses and turns can be significant.

5. Use of diagonals

Falling into the trap of movement, which is almost exclusively in lines parallel to the front of the stage, is all too easy. If this happens too often, the movement will be shallow and less interesting than it could be. It is far better to explore the whole space with crosses that go from downstage to upstage, i.e., from downstage left to upstage right. As a general rule of thumb, it is usually desirable to have at least a slight diagonal on most crosses. Many people who do drama in churches are working on a rather limited stage. One way to make the space seem bigger is through diagonal crosses that explore the whole area. And conversely, a space will seem smaller than it is if the movement is limited to crosses parallel to the stage edge.

It is also useful to place furniture on an angle, rather than setting it parallel to the front of the stage. If only a couch is used, I will generally angle it slightly. This, I think, is more interesting and creates, especially with the addition of a few other pieces (i.e., chair, coffee table, etc.) a more interesting and inviting environment, one which is dynamic as opposed to flat. Furniture is often needed in a sketch, but it also can be used to help create a more realistic environment for the action. Usually, however, we use only the furniture we need (if a chair isn't sat in, we don't use it). Since in our situation the sets are usually struck after the sketch is performed, we try not to use anything that isn't necessary. Thus we don't use additional furniture or props to help create atmosphere. With a few exceptions, we aim for economy of setting.

6. Having the right amount of movement

On ends of a continuum, movement can be either too static or too frenetic. Neither, of course, is desirable. The director must judge whether or not the amount of movement is appropriate. Sometimes in rehearsal a director and actors will have so much fun working out crosses and turns that they end up with a far too "active" sketch. If this is the case, the director, obviously, has to eliminate some of the movement. On the other hand, a director may find a sketch flat and unenergized in rehearsal, and would probably do well to add some movement.

Working Out the Blocking

Now that some principles and tools of blocking have been established, how does one go about the task of actually figuring out the blocking? One approach is for the director to pre-block. This means that prior to the first rehearsal the director makes blocking choices. These are then suggested to the actors in rehearsal. Another approach is for the director and actors together to work out the blocking in rehearsal. In this case the director does little or no pre-rehearsal work.

I strongly encourage pre-blocking, especially if a director is working with less experienced actors. The truth of the matter is that novice actors are probably not going to be of much assistance in figuring out the blocking. As has been discussed, they need a director to give them suggestions and thereby increase their confidence. I believe it is highly desirable for a director to "live with" a script prior to rehearsal and to think through character and blocking. Not only does such preparation indicate to the team that the director is prepared, but rehearsal is much more efficient. It takes a lot of time to experiment with different blocking. If one is doing a sketch, the basic blocking should be established by the end of the first rehearsal, which for us is usually about an hour and a half.

Some directors argue against pre-blocking because it assigns movement rather than encouraging actors to think of movement as an extension of their character. They believe movement given by a director risks looking like assigned blocking (because it hasn't been "owned" by the actors). Furthermore, these directors feel it is far better for everyone to make creative choices together, with the director having the final word. Such an approach, they maintain, produces better results. I believe these arguments have much merit.

> **Too many directors approach rehearsal without a game plan.**

But, again, if one is to work this way, it necessitates actors who have some experience. The more experience, the better the results of a group creative process.

I argue that, especially on the amateur level, directors need to be providing more, not less. Too many directors approach rehearsal without a game plan, looking to their actors to have answers. But actors need to be led! Actors want directors who know what they're doing and have a plan. Pre-blocking will seem like "assigned movement" only if it is unmotivated movement or if an actor has not been brought to an understanding of what the motivation is. Blocking which is suggested to actors can be "owned" as easily as blocking they come up with themselves. And if some blocking choices of the director cannot be believably executed by an actor, then they need to be changed. Furthermore, even a director who pre-blocks needs to be open to suggestions for movement by actors.

In reality, most directors use a combination of both approaches, depending on the level of experience of one's cast.

Whatever the approach, what is important is that the director is prepared and runs an efficient and enjoyable rehearsal that accomplishes what it needs to.

Crafting a Moment

I remember my first experience seeing the musical *Les Misérables*. I was in London, in one of the worst seats in the house, yet through the course of the production I experienced many moments that touched me deeply. But the one that literally sent chills up my spine was the incredible chorale "One Day More" that closes the first act. Evidently I was not alone, for it was the only time I have experienced cheers and a standing ovation from an audience only halfway through a show!

> **The difference between something working and not working is often minute.**

"Moments" happen when an audience member, through strong identification and a significant empathetic response to the character(s), is moved by what he sees. Moments seldom just happen; they are crafted. And theatre practitioners put significant effort into their creation, for such moments can be potentially transformational.

A large part of a moment is dependent upon the script. It's the script that has to "get us there." Once determined that a script has potential, then it is up to the actors and director to maximize the impact.

The difference between something working and not working is often minute. I'm amazed by how one little detail can destroy a potential moment. If the line is said too slowly, without the proper pause, or if the lights fade too quickly, or not quickly enough—the moment is lost. Crafting a moment takes directorial fine-tuning; no detail is too small. Again, being off a few seconds in timing is all it takes to deflate potential.

In sketches the possible moments are frequently at the end. At Willow Creek we fairly often "package" a sketch and a song together. The right ballad can not only help create a moment but sustain it as well. Sometimes it is effective to bring in musical underscoring during the last lines of a scene and then go directly into the song. At other times it feels better to have a few seconds of silence after the last line and then quietly bring in the music. But it's an inexact science. If a vocalist moves into place too quickly, if the pause before the music is a few seconds too long, or if the music intro comes in too briskly or is too "busy," the moment will be hampered.

Recently we did a sketch with huge moment potential. The script was strong, the ending touching. At the sketch's conclusion we transitioned directly into a song by cross-fading lights from the actress to the singer. But the introduction to the song was too long, forcing the actress to sustain action (surprised response to a letter) longer than was credible. Since the acting appeared a bit forced, the moment was largely lost. Yet the solution was an easy one—about eight seconds less of musical introduction.

A director needs to trust his instincts and make sure that all that goes into crafting the moment—light, music, dialogue—is well-rehearsed. Nothing can be left to chance. The dramatic power is in the details.

It's also important to give careful consideration to what follows a moment. This is a potential time for significant ministry because many in the audience will be in a vulnerable place. The rule of thumb is to simply pay attention to what just happened. In conferences when we've used a touching sketch to set up a guest speaker, we're often disappointed by how the speaker seems oblivious to what just occurred on stage. He gets up and cracks a joke when many have just had their hearts deeply stirred. It would be far better to be comforted with some pastoral words and perhaps Scripture. Or it might be desirable to experience a period of silence for reflection, or to be led in prayer, perhaps a guided one. The transition out of a moment needs to be gradual and handled with great sensitivity.

Coaching Actors

One of the great privileges of my life has been to see actors grow in confidence and in ability and then to have fulfilling ministry experiences. I love the process of development for the purpose of equipping others to serve God!

In order for the process to work well, the relationship between actor and director needs to be one of trust and safety. Some directors achieve results through intimidation, fear tactics, and power plays. While such approaches might produce short-term performance results, they are ultimately damaging to people. Far better are directors who seek to follow Christ's example, ones who serve, encourage, and build up their actors.

Actors need to see their director as an ally, as a person who is committed to making them look good, someone who is determined to give them an experience that is as fulfilling as possible. In short, actors should view their director as their biggest cheerleader.

Keeping Ego in Check

Perhaps the most destructive force to a performance ministry is inappropriate ego. None of us like working with prima donnas. And, sad to say, the church has its share of them. How unfortunate that the egotistical performer is almost a stereotype in our culture, a fact which gives a subtle kind of "permission" to up-and-coming performers that it's okay for artists to have an "artistic temperament." Unfortunately, for many the hallmarks of an "artistic temperament" are oversensitivity, self-centeredness, and rudeness. Obviously we need to do what we can to dispel such faulty thinking.

> **The relationship between actor and director needs to be one of trust and safety.**

One way to help keep individual egos appropriately aligned is through focusing on a good process. In fact, I think it is healthy to focus primarily on process instead of product. Though a good process usually produces a good product as well.

If we are product driven we are sending a signal to our teams that what ends up on stage is "everything." And if the product, which is public, is held up over process, which is not public, then it stands to reason that the soil will be fertile for ego growth. When this happens, the felt perception by actors is that the performance is all that really matters.

On the other hand, if we place value on the process of rehearsal, on the process of learning our craft together, and if we celebrate steps of growth, then ego will more easily be held in check. In short, we're about more, much more, than simply putting a good product on stage. I don't mean to make this sound simpler than it is. Sometimes, no matter what we say or what we emphasize, the "performance thing" is what is most important to members of our teams. We are, after all, a performance ministry. But, as leaders, we cannot lose sight of the fact that our attitude, our emphasis, which affect what our team thinks is most important, can either help or hinder the "ego problem."

> **Often inflated ego is an issue of actor insecurity rather than superiority.**

A further word on egotism. When it emerges on our teams, we need to deal with it. Wishful thinking will not make it go away. When we detect a prima donna attitude, we need to talk to the person and express our concerns. There is no need to attack. Simply offer an observation. Sometimes this is enough. People can be unaware of how they're being perceived. Often inflated ego is an issue of actor insecurity rather than superiority. Just talking with a team member about the issue can help. Sometimes, if after numerous conversations a person's attitude doesn't change, that person probably should be asked to leave the team. A bad attitude, as many of us have experienced, can cause much damage.

Perhaps the most significant factor in controlling the "ego problem" is good modeling on our teams. I'm very grateful for our key volunteers at Willow Creek because they model humility and servanthood. I thank God for the gift of these people! They are the ones who are setting the standard for new members coming on to our teams. When recruits come alongside veterans who exhibit true humility, that humility becomes very appealing and has a significant impact on their own attitudes.

Rehearsals

Directors need to view rehearsals as a top priority. This means that we're prepared, we accomplish our goal, we use time efficiently, and we approach the work with an attitude of enjoyment. In addition, we're sensitive to the needs of different actors, we challenge, speak the truth in love, and encourage. It's a tall order. But it's important because the key to a good performance is good rehearsal. For the novice, it is often challenging to figure out how much rehearsal is enough. This becomes clear with time and experience. At Willow Creek we usually spend about five hours in rehearsal per sketch. But this assumes performers of some experience. If your actors are just beginning, more rehearsal is merited.

We have two separate rehearsals. The first one, usually lasting about an hour and a half, is on Tuesday nights following our team time. The actors picked up the script the previous weekend when they attended church. They have looked over the script prior to rehearsal, but generally have not yet memorized it. The goal for the first rehearsal is to discuss the sketch and characters as well as establish the blocking. After a read-through, I'll ask questions such as: What's going on here? What's the sketch about? We'll also talk about characters. What is the conflict? What is the objective, or goal, of the characters? Objectives should always be described in terms of action, i.e., "to get my wife to admit she was wrong," "to vindicate myself by finding the evidence," "to win the argument at any cost." Helping actors to articulate what their characters are after gives them something specific to start with. The more specific, the better. During rehearsal, new layers of character are discovered, perhaps objectives are adjusted.

Maintaining the proper rehearsal "atmosphere" is the director's responsibility. A rehearsal should be enjoyable, even fun. There should be time for some laughter, with actors allowed to "cut up" some but, obviously, work needs to be accomplished. I've experienced directors on both ends of the continuum. Some essentially exert little or no control. While their rehearsals may be fun, after two hours virtually nothing has been achieved. Others "rule" with an iron fist and take the work so seriously that one is afraid to even smile. The work on drama progresses, but the rehearsal is stiff, uncomfortable, and not enjoyable. Obviously there needs to be a balance. It might be the tendency of beginning directors to be too lax and allow an excessive amount of "goofing off." When this happens a director needs to take control, say, "Okay, it's time to get to work," and make sure that happens. Ultimately, actors won't respect a director who is unable to accomplish the work required in rehearsals. Over time, with experience, a director learns when to have a loose hold on the reins and when to hold them tight.

Throughout rehearsals, and particularly the first one, the director needs to assist the actors in proper inflection, line interpretation, and in understanding the subtext. Proper inflection is often a problem for the novice and sometimes even for experienced actors. I'm amazed by how often this is a flaw in television acting. For example, the line "I'm responsible for her" can have three different meanings depending on which word is emphasized." If "I'm" is emphasized, the line means "I'm responsible for her, not you." If "responsible" is the accented word, the line means "I'm responsible, don't question my responsibility!" And if "her" is emphasized the line means "I'm responsible for her, not him." Thus, three different meanings with the same line, the changes being simply a matter of how words are or are not emphasized. Or take the question "Have you had enough to eat?" And the response, "Yeah." That one-word answer, "Yeah," can mean, "Great, I have," "I suppose," or "What's it to you?" It's all a matter of how it is said.

Proper line interpretation offers a similar challenge. Directors need to be sensitive to that which is literal and that which has a subtextual meaning. When a character says, "I don't want to go to the movie," what does she mean? Is the meaning literal, the person doesn't want to go to the movie because she's not interested or too tired? Or does the person not want to go to the movie because she wouldn't be caught dead with the person asking? If it is the latter, how much of that meaning is evident in the way the line is said, or how much is only part of the subtext and not clear from how the line is spoken? While the real reason a line is said may not be evident to the audience or to the other character—it stays subtextual—it is vitally important to the actor playing the part.

After some discussion of the script and characters at the first rehearsal, I like to get actors up and working rather soon. Too much "talk" can be to the detriment of performance, because there isn't enough time left to adequately rehearse the sketch. Before actually working on blocking, a ground plan needs to be presented, i.e., how furniture and props are arranged. In this first rehearsal I don't have the furniture we'll actually use, so we improvise with what is available, i.e., three chairs lined up to make a sofa. I suggest specific blocking, though I'm also open to suggestions from the actors. By the end of the first rehearsal my goals are to have the blocking figured out (though we may adjust it moderately at our second rehearsal) and to have the actors less dependent on the script.

The second rehearsal is in the afternoon, prior to our first service on Saturday night. We have another hour and a half, this time on stage with the furniture and props we'll use. No scripts are used during this rehearsal, so in the beginning actors will periodically call for lines. Some directors complain that it is challenging to get their actors to put down their scripts. But this is a director problem, not an actor problem. At Willow Creek our actors would never use a script in a second rehearsal. That's because we don't allow it. It's as simple as that.

This rehearsal is for polishing. We make sure the blocking works and appears motivated, we work on the rise and fall of action, and fine-tune the builds to the climax (see "Staging a Sketch," page 151). We also work on the details of characterization, making sure there is as much clarity and depth as possible. In this final phase of rehearsal, I want to see a performance level from the actors. Some actors want to hold back and only really "deliver" in performance. However, I want to see in rehearsal what will be on stage, so I coach to that end. During the last half hour of this rehearsal we add sound and light. We mic up (we use wireless lapel mics) and rehearse with any sound effects we might need. If it is a more complicated sketch for sound effects, we would add another fifteen minutes of rehearsal.

All of the lighting and sound needs have been requested the day before, at a production meeting. If special sound effects are necessary that may take time to find, I'll make the request as early in the prior week as possible. A sketch usually needs only area lights, but sometimes I'll want a special, i.e., a smaller pool of light to focus in on a character at the end. Before the final rehearsal, the lighting special is rough focused, leaving the fine focusing to be done while the actors rehearse.

After we leave the stage, we still have approximately two hours before the service begins. We take a break for a while, but generally spend a fair amount of time running lines and working on problem areas off stage. At Willow we have the advantage of performing four times, so we continue to fine-tune through the last service. Notes are given after each performance, and it is not unusual to change a line or make some cuts based on audience reaction. One has to be careful that the actors can manage the changes, but generally this isn't a problem as long as the changes aren't too extreme.

After the first service the programming staff, and frequently the teacher for that weekend, gathers for a mini-critique of the arts elements. Sometimes suggestions will be offered concerning the drama and music portions of the service. One person might say the sketch seemed slow, or a certain part or actor lacked energy, another might be confused by a line. From this feedback I make the changes I feel are appropriate. The programming team's reaction is important and valuable, since by this point they are far more objective than I am.

eight

Staging a Sketch

Directors and actors alike find much fulfillment in bringing words printed on paper to life. Applying the techniques of the director's craft to the task of creating an experience on stage that captivates an audience is not only rewarding, it's great fun! Much of the previous information in this book will, in this chapter, be helpful in the practical task of staging a sketch.

I've chosen the script *Feeling Opposition*, by Donna Lagerquist, because it provides a number of challenges. First, it's a sketch that does not have a lot of inherent movement—thus the challenge of creating blocking that not only assists in character definition but also "tells the story." Second, it provides some interesting character challenges. If not played correctly, the woman will appear annoying and the husband, an insensitive brute. The sketch will end up more sad than funny. In order for it to work, the right comic tone must be found. Also, the script is somewhat stereotypical, because it presents a female character who is overly sensitive and a man who is out of touch emotionally. The challenge is to create believable characters with whom the audience can identify, characters an audience will care about.

I remember when we came up with the idea for this sketch and were somewhat concerned about the stereotypical nature of the characters. We toyed with the idea of making the male emotionally in touch and the female disconnected. We decided to go ahead with the more typical scenario because we thought this would create the most audience identification. But we also wanted to experience in some way the emotional vulnerability of the male.

This sketch serves as a good example for staging because it involves only three characters in a simple setting. It demonstrates how to effectively use a few simple hand props. It also shows the connection between structure and staging, and how to gradually build the action to the climax.

What follows presents one approach a director could use in staging this sketch. I do not present it as *the* way to do it. Directors deal with material in different ways. The key, when approaching a script, is simply to make good choices that assist in telling the story.

Before beginning, let's review staging terminology. When directions are given to an actor to move "stage right" or "stage left," it means to the actor's right or left as they stand on stage facing the audience. When an actor moves toward the audience he is moving "downstage." When he moves away from the audience he is going "upstage." The terms downstage and upstage were developed during the Renaissance when stage floors were raked (lower in front, higher in back). So in the sixteenth century when an actor went upstage she literally went to a higher level; downstage meant she moved to a lower level of the stage. The term "beat" refers to a momentary pause.

The setting for our example sketch is a lawyer's office. It begins with a couple reviewing some paperwork at a table in the office, thus all that is really needed in terms of furniture is a table and two chairs.

Let's begin with Kate in the chair farthest upstage and her husband, Phil, in the chair to stage right. In this position, Kate is more open (or visible) to the audience, while Phil is somewhat more closed (his face is less visible because he sits to the side). As we will see, Kate is the character who is struggling the most, thus she is placed in the most "open" position. The lawyer, Carl Stinson, stands between them. A box of tissues is on the table.

NOTE: The material in bold is instruction from the director.

Stinson: **(Holding the document)** Okay, everything looks good ... all we need are a couple of signatures and everything's legal. **(He sets the document down)**

Phil: (cheerfully going to sign) Okay.

Kate: (grabs Phil's arm) Ah, Mr. Stinson, could we have a few minutes alone?

Stinson: (joking) Sure thing. Phil, outa here, will ya? Your wife wants to see me alone.

Kate: No ... I meant ...

Phil: Carl ... (both laugh, Kate doesn't. Stinson notices and then gets serious)

Stinson: (to Kate) Is there something wrong with the wording or ... don't you understand?

Phil: No, it's fine, and I think we've used enough of your time. **(He says this line as much to Kate as to**

Carl, as though, "come on, just do it." Now directly to Kate) Kate, just sign it.

Kate: (to Stinson) Please ... just a few minutes? **(She refuses to give in to her husband's pressure)**

Stinson: Sure, I understand. The finality of the paperwork and all can be a little more difficult than anticipated.... (to Phil) Happens all the time. **(He then turns and starts to cross right)**

Phil: That's okay, Carl **(Carl stops, turns, and crosses back)** Kate'll sign it as is.... **(to her, but a little through his teeth)** C'mon, Honey, he's a busy man, and we've been over this many times!

Kate: (to Stinson) **(Not giving in)** Please.

Stinson: **(He again crosses to the right, as though leaving)** Sure, I can give you a few more minutes. **(turns back)** After all, Phil, you did see that our phone system got up and running the same day I moved into this new building.

Phil: Yeah, how's it working?

Stinson: Great ... **(One step toward Phil)** well, there's a little glitch over at the reception desk, but...

Phil: Really? **(He stands up)** Let me take a look. (Kate clears her throat. Phil gets the point) Hey, I'll send a repairman first thing Monday, okay?

Stinson: Sure thing **(As he leaves, going out right)** I'm still working on those Bulls tickets. (He exits)

This section of dialogue comprises the EXPOSITION. It provides all the information we need to know: Phil and Stinson are friends, and Stinson is returning a favor with a legal service. We also discover that Stinson has previously said he'd try to get some Bulls tickets for Phil.

But at this point it isn't clear why Kate and Phil are in the lawyer's office. We really don't know what's going on. It is this device, a sense of mystery, which helps sustain audience interest through the exposition. It offers more than just background information. Perhaps the audience thinks it's a divorce situation, but then Stinson's joking about Phil's wife wanting to be with him makes little sense. In short, we're not sure what it is. And that's good.

Phil: **(Takes a step after Stinson to open up the scene somewhat, then turns to his wife)** So, what's up?

Kate: How can you be so cold and unfeeling?

Phil: Are you talking to me?

Kate: Yes! Laughing, talking about glitches in the phones and basketball. We're about to make a life-changing decision! **(she grabs some tissue, beginning to get emotional)**

Phil: **(Crossing to her, which is only a few steps)** Kate, I think you're getting a little overemotional about this.

Kate: Overemotional! We're talking about the future of our son!

Phil: **(He sits down, realizing this isn't going to be easy)** Kate, really . . .

Kate: I don't want Gerald and Mary to raise Tyler!

This line could be viewed as the INCITING ACTION. We now know that they're dealing with guardianship of their son, Tyler. This introduces the conflict we've already seen hints of. Notice how the conflict is underscored in these next few lines.

Phil: They won't.

Kate: (pointing to paper) They might! And they hardly know him!

Phil: Gerald and Mary are his aunt and uncle. It's only logical that they . . .

Kate: They don't love him!

Phil: Yes, they do!

Kate: Not like we do . . . not like Jenny Kritchen does!

Phil: Jenny Kritchen . . . our baby-sitter?

Kate: Yes, she *loves* him!

Phil: Honey, we can't name a fourteen-year-old baby-sitter legal guardian to our two-year-old son! That's crazy!

This section of dialogue starts the RISING ACTION after the inciting action. And it is the first BUILD, meaning it grows in intensity and pace, peaking at "That's crazy!" The short lines lend themselves to an effective escalation in energy. Now, for variety, the action levels off some and gets more relaxed, but only briefly.

Kate: **(Standing up [A], somewhat reflective)** I get crazy just thinking about him sleeping anywhere but in his little race car bed. **(she crosses away [B], down left a few steps)** And anyone else putting little Barney Band-Aids on his booboos, or someone else potty training him.

A   **B**

This is an example of breaking a line up into two separate moves. Kate first stands, careful to motivate the movement out of a sense of sadness and concern. Then, after she says the first line, she moves, as though somewhat lost in her thoughts. While she wouldn't have to stand and cross, getting her up helps provide visual interest.

Phil: **(with a laugh)** No one else is gonna want to do that! **(Kate turns abruptly, as though expressing "How can you say that?" The turn, without any line uttered, can communicate much.)** (Kate glares at Phil, he turns serious) **(he stands)** No one else is

gonna do it. **(Conciliatory, crossing to her)** We're signing our wills, not our death certificates!

Phil's line entails three specific blocking choices. He stays seated for the first line, stands for the second and crosses on the third.

Kate:　Well, I feel like we are . . . **(she crosses away right [A], in front of him on)** I don't want to sign. **(the cross is clearly motivated with the idea of "Leave me alone, I'm not going to sign.")**

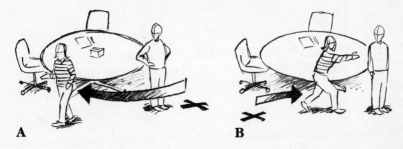

A　　　　　　　　　　　　B

(She ends up at some distance from Phil and stays facing away from him) I hate thinking about living without Tyler . . . **(she turns to him, beat)** or you. **(She says this next line emotionally, running [B] and throwing her arms around him.)** Oh, Phil, I love you so much!

This line indicates more clearly than any other how Kate's emotions are creating havoc. In the midst of thinking about not living with Tyler—which of course would only happen if she were dead—she is struck with the realization that she could lose her husband. It's important that this is played with the right heightened, comic tone. To underscore the humor, when Kate hugs Phil she catches him with his arms at his sides. The next few lines should level off somewhat since another build is coming up.

Phil: I love you too, Kate ... but why don't we go cuddle somewhere besides Carl's office?

Kate: **(As she continues holding him, looking up at him)** I never want to look at you lying in a casket!

Phil: (lightly) Oh, I'll try to be burned beyond recognition or something. **(This is like a blow in the solar plexus to Kate. She lets go of him, backing up a couple steps as she says)**

Kate: How can you say that?

Phil: I was trying to make you laugh?

Kate: I don't want to laugh, I'm sad.

Phil: **(He steps to her)** If you laugh, you won't be sad.

Kate: **(She crosses away left, in front of him)** But I am sad.

Phil: **(Turning to face her)** Well, you shouldn't be.

Kate: **(Turning to him quickly)** Stop telling me what I should or should not feel!

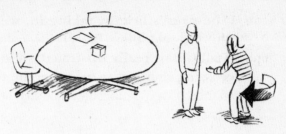

These three simple moves can work very effectively. He steps into her "space," she moves away a few steps as though saying "leave me be." Her turning back on "Stop telling me ..." is a good example of how a turn can help underscore and support the meaning of a line. This simple blocking is telling the story. This section is another nice series of lines to build. They should come faster and louder, peaking on the last one. This final line creates huge identification—many couples have been there—so it needs to be delivered with great punch and energy.

Phil: (growing frustration) **(Crossing to her)** Kate, we're only doing this because we're supposed to. It's wise, for you and me and Tyler ... just in case. Everybody should have a will just like everyone should have car insurance ... you just hope you never have to use it.

While the stage direction indicates this line should be said with "growing frustration," I think there is a better choice. Because much frustration is evident throughout the sketch, other attitudes must be found in order to give the performance variety. Since immediately before we built to a strong line with Kate gaining the upper hand, I think it makes sense for Phil to try a new approach with his wife. Clearly, he is not getting through. Thus, in this line he can be all sweet and nice. As he crosses and speaks to his wife, his tone is gentle. His motivation is to defuse the situation. (Stage directions provided in a script do not always need to be followed. If a director and actors, based on their interpretation, come up with a different approach, fine.)

Kate: **(She pauses briefly, taking in, we think, what Phil has said, then, flatly)** How comforting.

Phil: **(Phil is now really frustrated, so in an outburst, crossing right, away from her, he says)** Kate, I'm so tired of you getting all emotional at the least little thing.

The movement on this line and the energy with which it is said help to highlight it. And this is important, because the sketch's final comic punch is contingent upon the audience recalling that Phil said the line.

Kate: **(Crossing to the table, referring to the document)** What? The possible future of our son is a little thing?

Phil: **(Also crossing to the table, picking up a pen, trying to hand it to her, he's desperate)** C'mon, Kate, just sign it and I'll take you out for a late dinner and a little dancing.

Kate: **(Not taking the pen, looking out)** I just want to go home.

Phil: No dinner? No dancing?

Kate: I want to go and hold my baby (weepy) and tell him I love him . . . don't you?

Phil: I'd rather hold you. **(Tries to dance with her, still hoping the promise of dinner and dancing will get through to her)**

It would be a mistake to approach the line "I'd rather hold you" from a romantic angle. Phil is not interested in romance now, he wants to get the paper signed! The line needs to make sense in terms of his objective. He tries to force the dance because he desperately hopes the promise of a night out will get the task accomplished.

Kate: **(Not cooperating, pulling away)** Uh! Have you no feelings at all?

Phil: Obviously none you're interested in. **(He sits, defeated)** I guess I'm just being more practical about this.

Kate: "Mr. Practical." So what else is new! (pause) Would you cry if I died?

Phil: I suppose.

The way he says these two words is important. If he says
them too bluntly, he comes off as an insensitive brute. Furthermore, I think this approach would strain credibility. It would be
better to say the line like he's a bit preoccupied and caught off
guard. He is, after all, probably thinking, "How am I going to get
her to sign that document?" After he says this, she gives him "a
look." This jolts him back into reality.

> Phil: Yes, probably. (another look) **(He stands up [A])** Yes!
> Yes! I would definitely cry if you died. **(He crosses to
> her [B])** Look, Kate, I don't want to overextend my
> friendship with Carl. It's late. Let's just sign this one, and
> if we want we can change it later.

A   **B**

This line can be viewed as the CLIMAX, so it should be built
to with a great deal of energy. And this approach finally gets
results, Kate responds.

> Kate: (pause, beginning to give in) Promise?

This sudden change can be problematic for the actress. Why,
now, does she finally begin to capitulate? The assurance by Phil
that this isn't necessarily "set in stone" appears to be the point
that causes the breakthrough. But it must be played right, otherwise it will seem manipulated and not real. We have to see the
"lightbulb go on." The pause, during which there is this recognition, is very important to making her change work. Phil, perhaps a bit in shock, quickly picks up on it. The following can be
viewed as the FALLING-OFF ACTION.

Phil: (excited by the progress he sees) Promise . . . and I'm
         sure everything will look better tomorrow. (hands her
         the pen)

I like his holding the pen out, but she doesn't take it.

Kate: (lighter) I hope so. I guess it's a good thing we're
         both not emotional wrecks. We'd never get anything
         done. . . .

Phil: Yeah. **(He again tries to hand her the pen, an
         action which says "come on, just sign it!")**

Kate: (starting to sign) **(Rather than signing, she starts
         to take the pen, but doesn't)** Sometimes that prac-
         tical side of you drives me nuts. (throwing herself on
         him again) But I'd really miss it if it wasn't around.

This provides another comic moment. As Kate, once again
carried away by emotion, embraces her husband. It is fun to
experiment with this to find just the right way to do it. I like Kate
throwing herself over Phil's back as he leans over the table. The
embrace should be awkward and funny, not attractive.

Phil: (trying to extricate himself) Okay, okay. (guiding her
         hand to the paper) Before you get going again . . .
         (calls off) Hey, Carl! We're ready!

Stinson: (from offstage) I'll be right there, just finishing up
         some paperwork!

Phil: (she signs) **(objective achieved!)** Now that wasn't so
         bad, was it?

Kate: (not reacting) Did he say he was finishing the paper-
         work? Do you think he's gonna charge us? I thought
         he was your friend!

Phil: Honey, he's a lawyer. He thrives on paperwork.

Kate: But we've been here over four hours . . . if he charges
         us the . . .

Phil: Kate, will you relax? Stay calm, get a grip!

This last line is a setup, for Phil will soon lose his grip.

Stinson: (entering) Okay ... how did we do? (looks at will) Two signatures and a half a box of Kleenex left. Not bad!

Kate: I appreciate you giving us the extra time. I've never done anything like this before.

Stinson: No problem, I'll have Joyce put the finishing touches on it in the morning and drop it off Wednesday, okay?

Phil: Sounds great, thanks, Carl.

Stinson: (shaking hands with Kate and Phil) Sure thing, Phil. Kate.... I gotta run up to a client on the eighth floor ... so if you could just close the door behind you?

Phil: Sure!

Stinson: Oh, here. (hands envelope to Phil) Goodnight. (he exits). (Phil and Kate look at each other, shocked.)

At this point, in a rather atypical fashion, a new conflict is introduced. But it helps provide a twist at the end.

Phil: I don't believe it! (growing anger) I install a new phone system for him and he pats me on the back and says, "Stop in with Kate anytime and we'll put together a will for you" ... then he pats me on the back with a bill in his hand! (he hands Kate the envelope) Of all the tricks!

Kate: Phil, maybe we ...

Phil: **(He crosses a few feet stage left in front of Kate)** (mad) How can someone be so cold and unfeeling ... **(he turns and looks right where Stinson has just exited)** and sneaky, too! **(Again, a quick turn on the line underscores it nicely)**

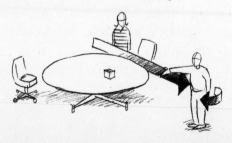

Kate: Maybe it's … (she begins to open the envelope)

Phil: (calling after Stinson, very upset) **(crossing right toward where Stinson has exited)** What's the matter, Carl, don't you even have a heart? Boy, did I have him pegged wrong. I have a good mind to rip out the whole system and …

Kate: (holding up two tickets) **(crossing toward him some)** Take it to the Bulls' game?

Phil: (still mad) How can you make jokes when … (sees tickets) Were those in the envelope? **(It's fun to have Phil still shout this last line. He's on a roll.)** (she nods, he's softer, humbled) No bill?

Obviously this is a fun section, and it serves to demonstrate that Phil, too, can get quite emotional when his "button" is pushed, in this case, his wallet! This change in character helps to "even the score" between the two of them. And, as is only appropriate, the final line gives Kate the upper hand.

> Kate:　(shaking her head) **(crossing to him, enjoying it all too much)** Ya know, I get so tired of you getting emotional over the least little thing!

This is a great closing line. It's not only comically satisfying, but it clearly signals the end of the sketch before the lights come down.

Assisting the Actors

The director is responsible for helping actors get a clear sense of their characters. In this sketch, Phil's objective, his goal, is quite obvious. He wants to get his wife to sign a will. It often helps to phrase the objective in strong action terms. The actor might say, "I must, through any means possible, convince my wife to sign that paper." Kate's objective, on the other hand, is a little more challenging to decipher. To say, "She doesn't want to sign" is not only a negatively stated objective, which is difficult to play, but it isn't very specific. Other possible objectives for the actress playing Kate might be, "I just want to be with my son," or "I refuse to deny my feelings to please my husband," or to state that more positively, "I must be true to what I'm feeling, whatever the result." Or maybe it is as simple as, "I must get my husband to stop this nonsense." Again, it isn't as though you are searching for the one correct objective. Different actors and directors will see different things. The point is to try to provide a focus, a "handle," with which your actors can work and develop consistent and interesting characters.

nine

Building the Future

Leading a vital drama ministry in the context of a local church can be not only exciting but also deeply fulfilling. I know that firsthand because I have had the privilege of doing it for many years. I, however, was not an "easy sell." When I was first contacted thirteen years ago about my interest in leading the ministry at Willow Creek, I, quite frankly, was not overly enthusiastic. I had been teaching for fourteen years in a Christian college and was concerned about how fulfilling a church drama ministry could be. I thought working in a church doing drama was something one of my students could do, but I had higher goals. I'm embarrassed now to admit that, because there is no higher calling than to assist in the building of churches that are true beacons of light to a desperate world. Willow Creek's senior pastor, Bill Hybels, and others have said that the only hope for the world is the church. I believe that. Now more than ever. To be a participant in the transformational work of Christ's church, to see people respond to grace, to witness the power of the Gospel to heal and change lives, to experience firsthand the joy of community with brothers and sisters who are united in heart and mission—now that is worth the investment of one's life and art!

Thankfully God worked on my heart and made clear to me, and to my wife, that His calling for the next season of life was to be a part of the arts staff at Willow Creek. And I've never regretted it.

I fear, however, that many are like I used to be. Most trained drama people who are Christians do not think of the church as their first career, or even ministry, option. This is because they often believe church drama is synonymous with poor art (much of it is) and therefore not really worthy of one's energy. Because many view the church as less than serious about drama, drama people who are serious about their art are not interested in working in the church. But with this kind of thinking, drama will never progress to the level where it will wield real impact in churches worldwide. There is a desperate need for trained people who have a vision for what drama can be in the church, for people who are willing to invest their best time and energy into the creation of drama that has the potential to transform lives.

> **There is a desperate need for trained people willing to invest time and energy in creation of drama that has the potential to transform lives.**

I know that many Christians with training in drama are attracted to theatre because they enjoy doing great literature. There is nothing wrong with this. The world's great dramatic literature needs to be performed and seen. I admit that I miss directing plays by significant historical and contemporary playwrights. But I also know that there are many out there doing Shakespeare, Ibsen, and Miller. And as noble as this might be, the church is crying out for trained, committed believers who have a vision for drama. And this doesn't necessarily mean the absence of secular literature, for this too can be part of a church's mission.

A Call for Vision

As we enter the next century, how exciting it would be if an increasing number of trained drama professionals viewed church ministry as their first choice and not as something they could fall back on in case the "real thing" didn't pan out. For this to happen, two things are needed: men and women with vision who are motivated by what can be and not by what presently is. And we need church leaders who not only affirm the value of drama but who also seek out qualified drama leadership—leaders they are willing to adequately compensate. Perhaps this second challenge is the biggest one.

But it is encouraging to see an increasing number of churches all over the world that are making a significant investment in drama ministry. If churches serious about drama can be aligned with trained people who are committed to ministry, there is no reason why drama programs cannot flourish. And each successful program will be emulated by others.

It sounds so easy. While "vision" is currently a popular term that motivates and inspires, carrying out that "vision" can be very challenging. When anything new or out of the ordinary is attempted, snags are met along the way.

Dealing with Snags

Perhaps one of the most challenging issues to deal with occurs when there is a difference of opinion as to the role of drama. Often a senior pastor, or someone else in leadership, may think the drama portion of a service should provide some answers. In short, they may have a rather narrow definition of what drama in a church should look like. As we've seen, drama is best at raising questions, at underscoring issues, and should not be used to preach. But when a pastor's previous experience has been with "Christian drama" that is message oriented, it is not surprising that he/she might take this position. When this happens, drama leaders need to be gentle persuaders. Help the pastor realize how drama and sermon can work together, each doing what it does best. And then work very hard to make sure that whatever drama is done sets up the message well.

In the start-up phase of a drama ministry, it might be wise to begin with drama that is somewhat more overt in message. We have some sketches that fall into this category, i.e., *Security Check, No Accident, The Story of Rachel, Maybe Someday, I Don't Want to Fight You Anymore, Life Cycle, Quiet Time, Prayer Perplexity, Plane Talk, Wait 'Til Half-Time,* etc. While a Christian perspective, either implied or direct, is more evident in these sketches, we have tried to avoid going too far in terms of message.

> **We need church leaders who affirm the value of drama and seek out qualified drama leaders.**

As a drama ministry develops, and the value of drama is more accepted by your pastor and congregation, one can begin to experiment with material that relates topically but is more secular in orientation. It's simply a matter of being wise. A drama director may be very attracted to material that is a bit more bold and challenging, but if she starts out with material like this, she may "turn off" people whose support and approval is needed in order for the ministry to exist.

Artists in the church need the permission of others to do what we feel God has called us to do. Some artists have a hard time with this. They assume the attitude, "This is my art, take it or leave it." These same people are unwilling to compromise and assume that their point of view is the only correct one. Frankly, the fact that we do not have more good art in the church is as much the fault of prideful, inflexible, purist artists as it is an unaccepting pastor or congregation.

Another challenge occurs when a pastor does not really understand what it takes for drama to be done well. For drama to work in the context of a service, there needs to be time to find or write a sketch that will connect with a particular sermon and then enough time for rehearsal. Pastors frequently don't know what they'll be speaking about very far in advance. At Willow Creek we need at least three and a half weeks' advance notice of a weekend's sermon topic. And more time is desirable. Sometimes a title is enough, but oftentimes we need more of the message's content. The challenge is that pastors are primarily concerned with the upcoming message and not the one that is still weeks off. Somehow this challenge has to be met, otherwise the desired strong connection between the pastor's message and the sketch will be lost. At worst, the drama portion will pose questions never responded to in the message. The result is like two ships passing in the night.

Thus pastors have to plan ahead further in order for this model to work. Some pastors maintain they want to be led by the Spirit and they resist being locked into a topic too far down the road. All of us want to have pastors who are attuned to the Holy Spirit's leading, but I don't think that means waiting until the last minute. I don't want this to sound sacrilegious, but I believe the Holy Spirit can give adequate notice. Yes, sometimes there will be a Spirit-led last-minute adjustment, and when this happens, we have to do our best to go with it. At other times, I think some pastors use "leading" as an excuse for lack of organization or effort. If we're on the same team, then adjustments need to be made in order to meet the various needs of the individual players. If this doesn't happen, we won't win the game!

Another sticking point between pastors and artists has to do with what I can only term "the inexact science of art." I wish that every week on stage at Willow Creek we had a classic drama presentation. But we don't. We hope that each weekend the sketch is effective and serves the purpose of the service, but that doesn't mean it's a "knock the ball out of the park" presentation. With drama there are so many variables, from script quality, to the way it is cast, to choices made by a director. When a classic happens, it's a gift. All these elements come together just right and we have a Mark McGwire weekend. And the more this happens—the more this kind of drama becomes standard—the more it becomes the expectation. So when drama does fall short, there can be tension.

Sometimes I think pastors and others in leadership believe that if artists just worked harder the results would be stronger. While that may be true in some cases, it is not as simple as that. I know many times I have worked harder to salvage a sketch that didn't quite reach the mark than I have with some "classics." The creation of art is about much more than the amount of work put into it. Examples abound in the secular world. How is it that a film director creates an award-winning masterpiece, only to follow it with another film that's widely regarded as a "dud"? How is it that the best sit-com writers can create a number of top-notch, funny episodes and then write one that falls far short? Is it just a matter of effort? No. Yet it is this inability to totally "crack the code" that makes attempting drama so challenging and enjoyable.

While excellence should always be the goal, pressure to continually hit a standard that is set too high can be very defeating to artists. When this happens the temptation will be to play it safe, to rely on formulas, and to avoid taking risks—all of which mean death for a vital drama ministry. But it also needs to be said that many churches do not set the mark high enough. Many pastors are too easily pleased.

When the arts are experimented with in churches, there is seldom a lack of reaction. And sometimes the reaction will be less than positive. Thus another snag. Some of the criticism that comes our way is valuable and constructive. But often behind the loudest voices are people who resist change or are simply suspicious of drama. It's important that we filter out the wrong voices. While we don't want to "blow off" negative comments, at the same time we need to realize that everyone's opinion is not of equal value. This does not mean that we avoid dealing with people whose comments appear somewhat misdirected. Over the years I have received many letters from people who express concern over everything from drama subject matter to the way a character was portrayed. Many of these people make valid points and I thank them for bringing the issue to my attention. Others, I feel, are off base. I write, or talk, to these people and express that I'm sorry they were offended, but I explain why I feel our approach was valid. I don't apologize unless I feel an apology is merited.

How do we know what's valid and what isn't? Sometimes this is obvious; other times I rely on the staff in programming for an objective perspective. Often it is apparent in the amount of reaction. If we receive numerous comments of a similar nature, then there is probably a valid concern that we need to pay attention to. On the other hand, if we get one letter, and a sketch was seen by thousands, it's important that I keep that response in proper perspective. Not that the reaction isn't valid, but I'm probably not going to change a script based on one person's opinion, especially if I, and my team, feel our approach was merited.

What's important is that all opinions, even those with which we vehemently disagree, are treated with respect. Again, artists can be overly sensitive and defensive. Our programs will not flourish unless we learn how to lovingly and winsomely deal with opposition or dissenting opinions.

On a personal level, it is important that we, as leaders, keep negative reactions in proper perspective. If we're at all sensitive, it is easy to be wounded by just one negative letter, even if we disagree with it. Often people who have been offended express themselves in harsh, hurtful words, and it is difficult not to take it personally and feel defeated by it. We want everyone to like what we do. But it doesn't work that way. In fact, if it does, it could mean we're shooting for the lowest common denominator and not achieving the real potential of our ministry. In short, we need to expect some negative reactions and learn how to deal with them in a God-honoring way.

Another snag is rooted in a practical reality. What we're doing is hard work. The longer we're at it, the more this becomes evident. The novice drama person is often surprised by this. After all, drama ministry seems like all fun and games. While it is enjoyable, if excellence is the goal, it is a lot of plain, old-fashioned work. It takes an enormous amount of tenacity, dedication, and sweat. I love the quote by pro golfer Gary Player, "The more I practice the luckier I get." It's the hard work of practice, not luck, that leads to success. Rather than luck, Christians sometimes rely on prayer and God's power to make up for a lack of work and preparation. It is far better to offer God the best of our work and dedication and then pray that He will bless those efforts.

Building a drama ministry is a step-by-step process. This is challenging for some strongly motivated leaders to accept because inherent in all of us is the desire to have what we dream of now. Many of us are not good at delayed gratification. But in the beginning stages of a drama ministry, as with anything else that is new, one is laying the groundwork, the foundation, upon which the future is built. We begin with fewer talented people than we'd like. We deal with resistance from those who don't understand the vision. We cope with inadequate resources and equipment. But rather than getting discouraged by the challenge, leaders with vision will see these snags as opportunities. The simple fact is that we need to start with what we have and believe that what we want, what we dream of, God willing, is "down the road." Leaders with vision will be encouraged by and hold on to each small step of growth—an actor who is clearly becoming more confident and natural, a sketch that really seems to connect with the audience, a team member with potential who expresses and demonstrates commitment, a "moment" that works, the addition of a third wireless microphone. These are all building blocks that ensure the future.

> It's the hard work of practice, not luck, that leads to success.

Rather than get discouraged by what is lacking, find what is working and celebrate that. It's a tricky business. We have to stay in the moment and be encouraged by everything that indicates growth. At the same time we need to look to the future and work toward even more quality and fulfillment than we have in the present. However, if we become too future focused, we will get discouraged by the mountain we have to climb, by all that we don't have, by all that isn't working as we had hoped.

All of us, in whatever stage of development, are working toward the future. At Willow Creek, after almost twenty-five years of drama ministry, we still have numerous unrealized dreams. And working toward them motivates me. Achieving a particular level of quality and then just maintaining that level is seldom fulfilling. Creative people are always thinking, "Okay, we did that, now what's next?" One of the great thrills of leadership is the realization that the future is gradually being realized, that what we hoped and prayed for is actually beginning to happen. It always seems to take longer than we thought it would, but when it happens, it is deeply fulfilling.

> **One of the great thrills of leadership is the realization that the future is being realized.**

Thankfully, ministries aren't built by our strength alone. The apostle Paul reminds us in 1 Peter 4:11 (NASB), "Whoever serves, let him do so as by the strength which God supplies; so that in all things God may be glorified through Jesus Christ, to whom belongs the glory and dominion forever and ever." He is the one who gives us the vision, the strength, and helps us navigate the challenges in order to bring glory to Himself.

Part of bringing glory to Himself is reconciling a fallen world. And we, as drama leaders, can be agents in that Great Commission. We have the privilege of not only living out the church in the community of our teams but also of playing a part in turning people's lives toward Christ. That's not just a hope, it's a reality. Churches all over the world are filled with people who have encountered their Savior and are growing in their faith because the Holy Spirit used the art of drama to break through their defenses.

After a Good Friday drama presentation two years ago, I received a letter of gratitude from a woman who was deeply impacted by what we did. In closing, let me share the end of her letter with you:

> You can't see our faces because of the lights, you don't know our names, you don't know where we have been or where we are struggling to go, but we are watching.
> Don't ever doubt that we are watching and that God may be preparing a heart right this minute to grow because of what you do.

And people are watching in your churches. Right now God may be preparing hearts for what *you* will do. May God bless you in your drama ministry.

Appendix

Drama Resources and Training

Acting Training

Spolin, Viola. *Improvisation for the Theatre*. Evanston, Ill.: Northwestern University Press, 1963.

Still the major resource book for improvisations.

Bernardi, Philip. *Improvisation Starters*. Cincinnati: Betterway, 1992.

Includes hundreds of character situations for improvisations.

Custer, Jim, and Bob Hoose. *The Little Book of Theatre Games*. Kansas City, Mo.: Lillenas Publishing, 1997.

A book of numerous drama games and improvs for actor training.

Shurtleff, Michael. *Audition*. New York: Walker and Company, 1978.

More than a book on auditioning, it presents a series of questions and principles that promote a deeper level of character exploration. A good book for both directors and actors.

Script Sources

Cloninger, Curt. *Drama for Worship,* vols. 1 and 2. Cincinnati: Standard Publishing, 1999.

Creative Resource Group, P.O. Box 1627, Franklin, TN 37065.

Offers a free drama catalogue.

Johnson Creative Enterprises, Paul and Nicole Johnson, P.O. Box 3027, Brentwood, TN 37027.

Sketch material similar to Willow Creek Community Church material.

Lillenas Publishing Co., Box 419527, Kansas City, MO 64141

Offers *The Worship Drama Library,* numerous volumes of sketches for enhancing worship, as well as other drama materials, i.e., Steve Trott's *Psychotherapy to Go,* 1996.

Pederson, Steve, ed. *Sunday Morning Live,* vols. 1–9. Grand Rapids: Zondervan, 1992–98. (Volumes 8 and 9, shared editorship with Mark Demel.)

Sunday Morning Live, videos, vols. 1–9. Grand Rapids: Zondervan. (European VHS videos in PAL format available through: Scripture Press, Raad Road, Amersham-on-the-Hill, Bucks HP6 6JQ England.

Each volume contains six Willow Creek drama sketches.

Poling, Debra, and Sharon Sherbondy. *Super Sketches for Youth Ministry.* Grand Rapids: Zondervan, 1991.

Thirty creative topical sketches for youth.

Willow Creek Direct, P.O. Box 3188, Barrington, IL 60011-3188. Phone: 800-570-9812. Fax: 888-922-0035. Also available through the Internet at: www.willowcreek.org.

Willow Creek Sketches. A free sketch catalogue is available.

Professional Organization/Training

Conferences

Christians in the Theatre Arts (CITA), P.O. Box 26471, Greenville, SC 29616; Tel: 864.271.2116.

A very good organization that brings together church drama people with those working in professional theatres and Christian college theatre programs. Sponsors one national and numerous regional conferences each year.

The Willow Creek Arts Conference. Offered annually. For information, write to: Willow Creek Association, P.O. Box 3188, Barrington, IL 60011-3188.

Books

Noland, Rory. *The Heart of the Artist: A Character-Building Guide for You and Your Ministry Team.* Grand Rapids: Zondervan, 1999.

An excellent book that challenges artists to a deeper level of Christlikeness. Chapters such as "Excellence versus Perfectionism," "Servanthood versus Stardom," "Proven Character," "Handling Criticism," and "Jealousy and Envy" provide challenging and helpful straight talk that is always rooted in Scripture.

Watts, Murray. *Christianity and the Theatre.* York, UK: Riding Lights Theatre, 1986. (Available from Marketing House, 8 Bootham Terrace, York &03 &DH, England.

A small book presenting an apologetic for theatre. It discusses the church/theatre dynamic, covering issues such as the predicament of a Christian actor.

Briner, Bob. *Roaring Lambs.* Grand Rapids: Zondervan, 1993.

Briner focuses on how we can be true salt and light in the culture-shaping arenas of society: television, movies, and the arts.

Fischer, John. *What on Earth Are We Doing?* Ann Arbor, Mich.: Vine, 1996.

Fischer's vision is of a church that impacts contemporary culture rather than a church that is a subculture unto itself.

Community/Small Group Resources

Books

Sheely, Steve. *Small Group Ice-Breakers and Heart-Warmers.* Littleton, Co.: Serendipity, 1994.

————. *Small Group Jump Starts and Soft Landings.* Littleton, Co.: Serendipity, 1997.

Sheely's two books offer numerous activities and probing questions that promote community.

Jones, Jerry D. *201 Great Questions*. Colorado Springs: NavPress, 1997.

Good thought-provoking questions for group interaction.

Hybels, Bill. *Interactions, Small Group Series*. Grand Rapids: Zondervan, 1996–1998.

Excellent small group real-life study guides.

Notes

Chapter One
1. Murray Watts, *Christianity and Theatre* (Edinburgh: Handsel, 1986), 8.
2. Peter Brook, *The Empty Space* (New York: Touchstone, 1996), 60.

Chapter Two
1. Frederick Buechner, *Listening to Your Life* (San Francisco: Harper, 1992), 104–5.
2. Philip Yancey, *Open Windows* (Westchester, Ill.: Crossway, 1982), 166.
3. Yancey, *Open Windows,* 166–67.

Chapter Four
1. Dr. Suess, *Yertle the Turtle and Other Stories* (New York: Random, 1986).

Chapter Six
1. Ken Gire, *Windows of the Soul* (Grand Rapids: Zondervan, 1996), 161.

About the Author

Steve Pederson

Steve Pederson, after teaching on the college level for four-teen years, became the director of drama at Willow Creek Community Church in South Barrington, Illinois, in 1986. He leads a drama team of thirty-five laypeople. Team members perform each week as part of Willow Creek's seeker services. They also frequently contribute to conferences both at home and abroad.

Pederson has traveled throughout North America and Europe as well as Australia and New Zealand for the Willow Creek Association, teaching and leading workshops on drama in the church.

He has an M.A. in theatre from the University of Minnesota and a Ph.D. in theatre from the University of Iowa. His dissertation on the staging of a fifteenth-century morality play was selected as Dissertation of the Year by the American Theatre Association. It was published in 1987 by UMI Research Press.

Pederson has been the primary editor of the *Sunday Morning Live* drama series published by Zondervan Publishing House.

He and his wife, Kathy, a professor at Wheaton College, live in Hoffman Estates, Illinois, with their two daughters, Kimberly and Kristin.

WILLOW CREEK
RESOURCES

This resource was created to serve you.

It is just one of many ministry tools that are part of the Willow Creek Resources® line, published by the Willow Creek Association together with Zondervan Publishing House. The Willow Creek Association was created in 1992 to serve a rapidly growing number of churches from all across the denominational spectrum that are committed to helping unchurched people become fully devoted followers of Christ. Membership in the WCA numbers over 4,000 worldwide.

The Willow Creek Association links like-minded leaders with each other and with strategic vision, information, and resources in order to build prevailing churches. Here are some of the ways it does that:

- **Church Leadership Conferences**—3½-day events, held at Willow Creek Community Church in South Barrington, Ill., that are being used by God to help church leaders find new and innovative ways to build prevailing churches that reach unchurched people.

- **The Leadership Summit**—a once-a-year event designed to increase the leadership effectiveness of pastors, ministry staff, volunteer church leaders, and Christians in business.

- **Willow Creek Resources®**—to provide churches with a trusted channel of ministry resources in areas of leadership, evangelism, spiritual gifts, small groups, drama, contemporary music, and more. For more information, call Willow Creek Resources® at 800/876-7335. Outside the U.S. call 610/532-1249.

- *WCA News*—a bimonthly newsletter to inform you of the latest trends, resources, and information on WCA events from around the world.

- *The Exchange*—our classified ads publication to assist churches in recruiting key staff for ministry positions.

- **The Church Associates Directory**—to keep you in touch with other WCA member churches around the world.

- *WillowNet*—an Internet service that provides access to hundreds of Willow Creek messages, drama scripts, songs, videos and multimedia suggestions. The system allows users to sort through these elements and download them for a fee.

- *Defining Moments*—a monthly audio journal for church leaders, in which Lee Strobel asks Bill Hybels and other Christian leaders probing questions to help you discover biblical principles and transferable strategies to help maximize your church's potential.

For conference and membership information please write or call:

Willow Creek Association
P.O. Box 3188
Barrington, IL 60011-3188
ph: (847) 765-0070
fax: (847) 765-5046
www.willowcreek.org

Live from your church, it s Sunday morning!

Sunday Morning Live
Steve Pederson, General Editor

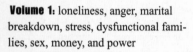

There's no more powerful tool to reach the unchurched than drama. And with the *Sunday Morning Live* series, you have the materials to act on it!

These Willow Creek-tested sketches raise questions, they make their audience laugh—or cry, and they act as a "set up" to the message given by the pastor, opening the audience to hear God's Word.

Volume 1: loneliness, anger, marital breakdown, stress, dysfunctional families, sex, money, and power
Book: 0-310-59221-6
Video: 0-310-59339-5

Volume 2: prayer, marriage, fear, tithing, and the Resurrection
Book: 0-310-61361-2
Video: 0-310-59549-5

Volume 3: witnessing, compassion, grace, and ambition
Book: 0-310-61441-4
Video: 0-310-61479-1

Volume 4: salvation, anger, rebellion, marriage, resolving conflict, abortion, God's presence, pace of life, and control
Book: 0-310-61531-3
Video: 0-310-61539-9

Volume 5: adultery, consequences of sin, prayer, evangelism, cults, broken families, personal finance, and trust
Book: 0-310-61541-0
Video: 0-310-61549-6

Volume 6: marriage, temperament, stereotypical church experiences, purity of thoughts, perils of power, serving two masters, and faith grounded in reason
Book: 0-310-61551-8
Video: 0-310-61559-3

Volume 7: having children, family relationships, personal responsibility, motherhood, eating disorders, and generosity
Book: 0-310-22156-0
Video: 0-310-22244-3

Volume 8: decision-making, facing fears, legalism, prayer, learning disabilities, and generosity
Book: 0-310-22157-9
Video: 0-310-22245-1

Volume 9: poverty, God, sisters, father-daughter relationships, "luck," and old age
Book: 0-310-22158-7
Video: 0-310-22246-X

Find *Sunday Morning Live* at your local Christian bookstore.

We want to hear from you. Please send your comments about this
book to us in care of the address below. Thank you.

ZondervanPublishingHouse

Grand Rapids, Michigan 49530

http://www.zondervan.com